THE BIG LIE

www.transworldbooks.co.uk
www.transworldireland.ie

THE BIG LIE

Who Profits from Ireland's Austerity?

Gene Kerrigan

TRANSWORLD IRELAND

TRANSWORLD IRELAND
an imprint of The Random House Group Limited
20 Vauxhall Bridge Road, London SW1V 2SA
www.transworldbooks.co.uk

First published in 2012 by Transworld Ireland,
a division of Transworld Publishers

A CIP catalogue record for this book
is available from the British Library.

ISBN 9781848271500

Addresses for Random House Group Ltd companies outside the UK
can be found at: www.randomhouse.co.uk
The Random House Group Ltd Reg. No. 954009

The Random House Group Limited supports the Forest Stewardship Council (FSC®),
the leading international forest-certification organization. Our books carrying the
FSC label are printed on FSC®-certified paper. FSC is the only forest-certification
scheme endorsed by the leading environmental organizations, including Greenpeace.
Our paper procurement policy can be found at www.randomhouse.co.uk/environment

Typeset in 11/15½pt Ehrhardt by
Kestrel Data, Exeter, Devon.
Printed and bound in Great Britain by
CPI Group (UK) Ltd, Croydon, CR0 4YY.

2 4 6 8 10 9 7 5 3 1

Arrive it will, the time, O Breanuin, when you would grieve to dwell in Ireland . . . The powerful will oppose the poor with false law and perverted judgements; lying will overflow the country . . . and the aged will mourn the times they shall have lived to see.

— St Colmcille, AD521–97

This'll sound controversial, but . . . I think rich people might be lying to us about how good the free market and privatization are.

— @chris_coltrane, 6 March, AD2012

For Cathleen Kerrigan,
with an apology from my generation,
to your generation,
for letting those fools
do what they did

Contents

Part Two: The Slow Death of the Old Politics

Voices

What This Book is About

THIS ECONOMIC COLLAPSE HIT us with bewildering speed and cut deep into our lives. And it's been obvious from the beginning that our leaders have been telling us fairy tales. The fairy tale changes as the crisis deepens. At first it was all about getting credit flowing, then it was all about balancing the books, then it was all about confidence. Eventually it became all about how smart it was to do whatever the grim lads from the European Central Bank in Frankfurt tell us to do.

We seek leadership from our politicians – but one crowd condemns the other shower; then they get into office and do precisely what the other shower was doing.

The official cover story is in shreds.

This book tries to figure out what's really going on. It isn't an exhaustive history of the crisis, it isn't about how we might save the banks, or how we might save the euro, or how we might leave the euro. It's not about how we might write a better budget or how we might get the deficit down to less than 3 per cent.

It's an alternative view of the crisis.

It's about the great majority of us who weren't playing the gambling games that created the mess. It's about what's being done to us, who is doing it and why. It suggests that some are benefiting from the austerity policies, while the rest of us lose.

It doesn't seek to recruit anyone to a programme of action; it describes how I think things work, where this crisis came from and perhaps where it's going.

Part One, *How the Old Politics Brought the Country to Its Knees*, gives an alternative view of how and why the crash happened, and the national and global politics that created the mess.

Part Two, *The Slow Death of the Old Politics*, deals with the repeated failures of the old politics to put Humpty Dumpty together again – and the role of austerity in turning a crisis into a catastrophe. It examines the failure of the rest of us to prise the cold, dead fingers of the bankers from our economic throats.

The book is not about economics. But economics is an important means of measuring one aspect of a political circumstance. And, these days, economics is too important to be left to the economists. Just as politics is too important to be left to the politicians.

So, the book embraces economic data gathered by the experts, but it draws a layperson's conclusions from that data – with a layperson's assumptions and preconceptions. I, of course, am wildly under-qualified for dabbling in economics. But given the record of the economists, I'm not bothered about that.

One crucial tool for understanding any crisis is to recognize that we don't all have the same problems. If you're on €20,000 a year, another government charge on top of the charges they've already heaped on to us can affect your living standards. Even those earning two or three times that will feel the effect.

If, on the other hand, your salary is €200,000 and you get a €40,000 bonus on top of that, all those charges are loose change.

People with huge salaries and pensions, people with property and share portfolios, government ministers and financial consultants all have problems of their own – and good luck to them. But the rest of us need to be aware of those people who are solving their problems by creating new problems for the rest of us.

We are not all in this together.

Much of what is told to us by politicians, bankers and their highly paid experts is self-evidently untrue. In order to persuade us to go along with one policy or another, they spoof, in meaningless phrases designed by their spin doctors: *We must stay at the heart of Europe*; *I've got a five-point plan*; *We've turned the corner*; *We all partied*; *Frankfurt's way*; *Not another cent for the banks*; *There is no alternative*; *The only game in town*; *Mustn't play the blame game*; *We're meeting our targets*; *We are where we are* . . .

And their pet experts and cheerleaders nod wisely.

The book's point of departure is that, at every stage of the crisis, we've been subjected to the Big Lie technique. The principle of the Big Lie was laid down by the Nazi propagandist Joseph Goebbels: 'When one lies, one should lie big, and stick to it.'

The Big Lie stands the truth on its head. It must be delivered with conviction, it must be repeated relentlessly and backed up by a range of nodding accomplices in the establishment.

People question small lies, because they can measure that kind of lie against their own experience. The Big Lie is so over-whelming, and it's so loudly endorsed – and believed – by such a range of eminent people that it's often swallowed whole.

To understand the foolish policies that dominate our lives, we have to explore their roots – globally and within Ireland. So, we examine how the Dáil and the media became full of mindless free-market extremists and their cheerleaders. And how the country became laden down with under-regulated bankers. And how, after the crash, the same thought-free culture led to the destructive austerity policies that crushed living standards for many and deepened the crisis.

When they were creating the insane conditions that led to the crash, they shared a view of the world – the politicians, the property speculators, the bankers, their consultants, their economists and their media cheerleaders. They still shared that view of the world after the crash. They share it still, despite the mess they've made since the collapse in 2008.

This view of the world led them to seek to restore things exactly as they were – with all the inequalities, the madness and the cruelties in place. It's the world they know, the world they believe works best. And – perhaps this is not a coincidence – it's the world that personally benefits them enormously.

From that view of the world, it made sense to transfer the bankers' gambling debts on to the backs of the rest of us – and to impose austerity policies to balance the books.

We examine what that world view is and where it came from. And where it's taking us.

As the recession bit hard, more people began to question the dominance of the austerity cult. In the final section of the book, under the title 'Voices', we include some of that questioning – writings and speeches by two poets, a teacher and the Ballyhea marchers.

A whole range of respectable people tell us there is no alternative to their austerity policies. And that the Big Lie, in their view, is a form of truth. Because a world in which they and their fellow travellers aren't grossly rewarded for their imagined talents is beyond their understanding. These people don't just tell a Big Lie, they live it.

There was a Big Lie behind the notion that ploughing billions into the shell of the banking system would 'get credit moving'. And another Big Lie behind the claim that the private debts of Irish, French and German bankers are 'our debts'.

The result: pain for those least able to bear it and a massive burden of debt lifted from the backs of the bankers and their patrons – and piled on to the backs of the citizens.

In crucial decisions, the elites are treating democracy as an optional extra. The affairs of this country are increasingly overseen not by elected politicians but by unelected officials in Frankfurt, Brussels and Washington. The hard-fought gains of social democracy, won by generations of ordinary people, are being pared away.

Far from making things better, the foolishness of the years since the collapse in 2008 has plunged the Eurozone into chaos and put the future of the European Union on the agenda.

Most of the public discussion of this crisis has been conducted over our heads, between elites – in jargon that sounds like economic theory. In truth, it's the nervous chatter of the cheerleaders of wealth.

They wrap the green flag around themselves, calling for sacrifice and patriotism, while they hold on fiercely to every perk and privilege.

They would rather sink the ship than compromise on their first-class quarters.

This book aims to answer the Big Lie with an array of small truths.

Part One

How the Old Politics Brought the Country to Its Knees

1

The Fairy Tale

B Y NOW, THEY CAN recite the fairy tale in their sleep.

Politicians, their media fans, tame economists and hired mouthpieces use the fairy tale to explain what happened. Like all stories, the details can be changed from time to time, but the basic fairy tale about the Celtic Bubble, the crash and the recession is pretty consistent.

And it goes like this.

Once upon a time, the Irish people threw off the shackles of the past that held us back. We began to work hard, to innovate, to find within us the talents we always had but which had been suppressed or neglected for too long. In the bad old days, you see, the Brits held us back, or perhaps the Catholic Church stifled our innate talents.

Whatever it was, once we threw off the yoke of oppression we became 'a nation of entrepreneurs'.

We began 'punching above our weight'.

We loved saying that.

'Punching above our weight'.

Those four words explained so much. We were still a small

country, with the intimacy and the charm of small countries, yet we were up there with the big guys.

Punching above our weight.

The economics that underlay all this remained hazy. There was no shortage of economists who felt free to expound on the roots of the miracle, but never convincingly. And they were usually working for banks or estate agents. When it came to explaining how a basket-case economy was suddenly being touted as an example for the rest of the world – well, there were a lot of gaps in the story. And an element of fairy dust.

Anyone suggesting that this might be a problem was a begrudger. And we all knew what to do with begrudgers.

Now, when a company bought or built a new building it wasn't just accommodation they wanted, they wanted to make a statement. It had to be state of the art, it had to be world class. Money was no problem; it was cheap to borrow. And people heading world-class companies needed rock-star salaries and bonuses.

Our rampant entrepreneurs bought a rake of prestigious London properties. For some, it was the ultimate victory – the peasants taking over the Big House. We discussed such triumphs ('Hey! Johnny's gone and bought Battersea power station!') with the same pride we displayed when Seamus Heaney won the Nobel Prize or Roddy Doyle the Booker.

And when anyone looked around at the Ireland we all knew still existed – with the lengthy hospital waiting lists, the Accident and Emergency chaos, the prefab classrooms, the ghettoes and the potholes – well, that just meant we needed to 'reform' some outmoded ways of doing things. And we'd get around to that in the by-and-by.

People might now and then become angry about something – maybe an A&E unit where the nurses were run off their feet and a relative had to wait twelve hours to be seen. Or another relative had an important operation postponed three times, in a hospital where the Department of Health never got around to replacing the beds they closed in the 1980s and 1990s.

But, hey, take a chill pill. Within the Celtic Bubble you could find any number of places in which to relax, while a cheerful barista offered you one of four sizes of eight versions of beverages our parents never dreamed of sipping, poor buggers.

Of course there were faults, the fairy tale admitted, but only losers dwell on the negatives. There was a lot done, and some more to do.

Then, according to the fairy tale, even as our courageous entrepreneurs climbed new heights, our new kick-ass nation was being undermined from within. They caricature this as: careless bankers lost the run of themselves; the regulators took their eye off the ball; and the politicians never noticed.

Even then, everything might have been all right if it wasn't for the bloody Americans.

The fairy tale explains how the Yankee bankers sold a lot of mortgages to poor people, who couldn't pay them, so their banks got into trouble. Then the George W. Bush government made a big mistake. When Lehman Brothers was going bust, Bush should have propped it up, say the people who know things. Instead, George W. and his people decided to let it go under, which caused no end of bother.

Credit froze right throughout the global banking system, at a time when the Irish housing market was slowing down and the grey, dreary waves of recession were lapping at our shores.

Oh, dear. Perfect storm.

Brian Cowen and Brian Lenihan were overwhelmed by it all, the fairy tale says, and they only had a few hours to make a decision – and they made the mistake of guaranteeing every cent the bankers borrowed from their fellow bankers abroad.

Most of all, the state had gone deep into debt, spending far too much. Now, we couldn't pay our bills, the cost of borrowing went through the roof and – the shame of it – we had to be rescued by the IMF and our friends in Europe.

This involved some harsh measures, some tough decisions, but that's what happens when a country loses sovereignty.

And we're all in this together.

Tough as it is, the only thing we can do is knuckle down, take our punishment. We'd had the fun, now it was time to pay the bill.

Fianna Fáil paid the price of its failure, the new government came into office – but their hands were tied.

There was a 'big hole' in the public finances, and the only way we could fill it was by kowtowing to the European Central Bank – and the ECB said that a lengthy blast of austerity would straighten things out.

No choice, you see.

But, if we all pull together and do our penance for our sins, we will eventually achieve a state of grace.

The fairy tale said it was just a matter of simple arithmetic. The amount of money collected in taxes was X. And it cost X plus Y to run the country. So, we had to borrow the Y.

But why are we paying billions to the bondholders and . . .

Ah, that's about confidence.

We have to generate confidence in our ability to pay back the money we will borrow in the future. And we do that by paying bondholders for the money we borrowed in the past.

But we didn't borrow it.

No, but they were Irish banks that borrowed it and – look, sure didn't Cowen and Lenihan think up that unfortunate guarantee . . .

But we've been paying billions in unguaranteed bonds and . . .

Look, this is complicated stuff.

Trust us. We know what we're doing.

Besides, our friends in the EU are giving us all sorts of concessions: money at cheap rates, the use of promissory notes – they can't do enough for us, God bless them.

And the thing that matters more than anything else is that – if we do as we're told – we'll eventually get our sovereignty back. We'll wave goodbye to the ECB and the IMF. We'll be free again!

The great thing about the fairy tale is that it uses bits and pieces from real life to prop up the fantasies that are woven through it. Fantasies and downright lies.

When we tell fairy tales to children they work because the children want to believe in dragons and princesses, in villains and heroes and magic; they want to see the world as black and white, easy to understand, with evil punished and good rewarded.

For the same reason, we want this infernal economic catastrophe to make sense. And when people in authority hold up a map that shows where we are and how we can escape from Oz and get back to Kansas, it's tempting to believe their fairy tale.

After all, they want what we want, don't they? Freedom, a return to prosperity.

Trouble is, they've been telling us fairy tales for almost five years now, and with each telling the story becomes more threadbare.

We took them seriously, the fairy tales, and the tired old political has-beens who told them. We wasted time, giving each changing tale a fair hearing. We allowed things to get much worse – to the point where the country is far more broken than it was in 2008.

The time for comforting fairy tales is long past.

We are where we are.

How did we get to where we are?

And where is the tired, old, failed politics trying to take us?

2

Playing with Tiger

THE AUCTIONEER SAID THAT the bidding would start at £100,000. It was a hell of a lot to ask for a single game of golf. But this was no ordinary game of golf, this was no ordinary charity auction, and these were no ordinary people being asked to bid.

Someone obligingly kicked off: 'One hundred thousand.'

The charity auction was held in County Limerick, and the game would be played at the Isleworth Country Club, Orlando, Florida. The successful bidder would get to play with the man then acclaimed as the greatest golfer in the world, 24-year-old Tiger Woods. Woods would team up with his friend and fellow pro Mark O'Meara. The successful bidder could bring three friends. A six-ball, over eighteen holes.

Soon there was a second bid: 'Two hundred thousand.'

And another.

Auctioneer Philip Myerscough, a veteran of Goff's bloodstock sales, didn't blink.

'Bid four hundred thousand pounds.'

It was the evening of Tuesday, 11 July 2000. That year was the borderline between the Celtic Tiger boom and what was to follow. There had been several years of economic growth, a big increase in employment – and a surge in confidence. What would happen in the years ahead would lead to frenzied money-grabbing, followed by dramatic collapse and a country loaded with crushing debt.

But that evening was a splendid indulgence by some of the richest and most powerful figures from the wealthiest, most self-confident Irish generation ever. Word got out in bits and pieces, of course – and it is from such evidence that we can stitch together an account of that evening. But this wasn't an occasion of vulgar boasting, it wasn't designed for PR purposes to impress the rest of us. This was a private gathering of an elite, financial and political, in a time of triumph, to raise a lot of money for good causes. It could also be seen as a celebration of wealth.

The auction was the climax of a two-day event, the third J.P. McManus Pro-Am Invitational Golf Tournament. It was held at the end of a banquet in a marquee tent in the grounds of Adare Manor. Millions would be raised for charity that evening.

The host for the Grand Banquet, and sponsor of the two-day charity event, was John Patrick McManus. Although a resident of Geneva, he was born in Limerick, retained a real affection for the area and maintained a mansion on 400 acres there.

It was all here, the seeds of Ireland's future: the rich men, the politicians, the celebrities. What the rest of us saw, perhaps, was a celebration of money, of absolute self-assurance – the politics, the economics and the culture of Celtic Tiger Ireland coming into its own. The previous seven or eight years had seen terrific growth – in money, in confidence. The next eight years would see an explosion of money.

You could measure the progress of Celtic Tiger Ireland in J.P.'s golf tournaments and charity auctions. The first Pro-Am sponsored by McManus took place back in 1990, when J.P. was merely rich.

It was a modest affair, with players from Ireland and Europe. It raised £2.1 million for charity. So successful was the tournament, McManus went on to host one every five years.

By 1995, J.P. was very rich, and his business interests and personal connections had spread. Three golfers from the US PGA circuit attended. The event raised almost £4 million. Let one of those present, pop singer Chris de Burgh, set the scene for that 1995 J.P. McManus Pro-Am Golf Tournament and Charity Banquet:

'I went to an event in Limerick, run by a guy called J.P. McManus. He has had two big golf classics, and these are totally remarkable because this is a man, a very wealthy man, who started life as a bookmaker and then got involved with all sorts of other business deals – but he's also extremely supportive of charity . . . Anyway, he had a two-day golf classic, in which I played with Christy O'Connor Jnr and various friends, including Robert Sangster and Charles Benson, a friend of his.'

By now, J.P. and his friends were held in great esteem in political circles. Here's Chris again. 'At the gala dinner, they had politicians falling out of your ears. There was the Prime Minister, the ex-Prime Minister, the Opposition Leader and many, many famous people.'

There was an auction at that year's banquet, too. One of the items on offer was an illustration, featuring caricatures of the Pro-Am's leading players. It was bought by Michael Tabor, for half a million pounds.

Originally from London, now living in Monaco, Tabor was – like his great friend J.P. McManus – a former bookie. And Tabor owned a horse called Thunder Gulch, which had recently won the Kentucky Derby. Two months earlier, McManus had asked de Burgh, as a special favour, to write and record a song called 'The Ballad of Thunder Gulch', celebrating the horse's win.

And that evening in 1995, when the charity auction ended, Chris de Burgh took the stage and sang the song he had written to commemorate Thunder Gulch's win. Michael Tabor was – de Burgh said later – 'very emotional indeed'. J.P. McManus presented Tabor with a professionally produced recording of Chris and a band performing the song.

This unexpected gift for Tabor was typical of the amount of detail that McManus put into his tournaments. There was nothing that Tabor wanted that he could not afford, but for McManus to commission a famous pop singer to write a song about one of the highlights of Tabor's life was to demonstrate an impressive amount of thought and friendship. It was this kind of consideration that sent people away from the Pro-Am singing McManus's praises, resolving to come back next time, spreading the word among their peers in wealth.

Five years later, advance comment on the 2000 Pro-Am suggested it might top the £4 million raised in 1995 by at least half a million pounds. By now, the J.P. McManus tournament was a significant event on the golf calendar. That year, thirty-six top golfers, including Tiger Woods, turned up.

'Six hundred thousand.'

Peter Myerscough accepted the bid.

So star-studded was the list of players that it provided an irresistible temptation for wealthy amateur golfers to hang out with the greats of the game ('Listen, I'd love to do lunch, but I'm hitting the fairway that afternoon, Tiger Woods is in town for a few days').

Not everyone on the advance list of players prepared by the organizers could make it, but the list promised many of the leading business people of the day: Denis Brosnan (his wealth raised in the food business), Gary McCann (bananas), Michael Smurfit (cardboard) and John Magnier (horse semen). And there were bankers present, as well as financier Dermot Desmond. There were sporting people galore, many from horse racing, along with UK Premiership stars such as Alex Ferguson, Martin O'Neill and Gary

Lineker. Over the years, showbusiness personalities from Brendan Grace to Hugh Grant turned up to swing a club, as well as such business stars as Denis O'Brien. About seven hundred people attended the 2000 banquet and auction – including many of the business people and politicians who would feature in the events of the next stage of the Celtic Tiger phenomenon.

A nod, a gesture, another bid for the game with Tiger Woods.

'Bid eight hundred thousand pounds.'

Mark O'Meara was on the stage, near the auctioneer. 'At that price,' he wisecracked, 'we'll throw in a free lesson!'

Another gesture from someone in the audience.

'Bid one million pounds!'

Stunned, O'Meara quipped: 'And we'll throw in a free lunch as well!'

Two more top-up bids of £200,000 each closed the bidding, and the eighteen-hole game with Tiger Woods and Mark O'Meara was knocked down for £1.4 million.

Just over two months earlier, on 1 May, wealthy Americans had bid in another charity auction, with the same prize – eighteen holes with Tiger Woods at Isleworth. The successful team of four bid $204,000.

This time, the prize went to Joe Lewis, a friend of Dermot Desmond and, like his friend J.P. McManus, an extremely wealthy currency trader. Lewis began life in London and now lived in Bermuda. Though he wasn't Irish, his life and wealth were interwoven with a set of Irish-born people. He and they moved seamlessly across national borders, defined not so much by their passports as by their wealth.

That golf game wasn't the only prize the rich jostled to buy that evening. A Jack Yeats painting, *The Cataract*, went for £1 million; a couple of tickets for Wimbledon, £80,000. A specially commissioned piece of Tipperary Crystal, signed by golfers and businessmen, went for £1.4 million; a flag from the 2000 US Open at Pebble Beach, signed by Tiger Woods, £1 million. Woods, who won the tournament (twelve under par), was reported to have donated his prize to the charity fund.

The tournament and the auction that evening raised £19.8 million for charity – a giant leap from the £4 million raised in 1995. Five years later, in 2005, at the height of the Celtic Tiger bubble, the event would raise €31 million.

The gathering of the rich golfers can be seen as a victory party to celebrate the coming of age of Entrepreneurial Ireland. And just as the event could call on golf stars, so it could rely on the attendance of the political classes, including Taoiseach Bertie Ahern.

Propelled by a sudden surge in wealth, Ireland was well on the road to absorbing new values, and the great banquet of the New Gentry was a significant landmark on that road. Given the terrible things that had been done to Irish people in the name of traditional values, the notion of a New Ireland, with new values, was not necessarily a bad thing.

But there's an old saying about frying pans and fires.

The values that had come to dominate this new Ireland weren't sucked from anyone's thumb. They emerged from the events of previous decades – here and internationally.

3

The Politics behind the Celtic Bubble

IT WAS ALL BERTIE Ahern's fault. And Brian Cowen's, too. And Sean FitzPatrick, of course.

In any disaster, it's tempting to blame one or two people, with a few walk-on parts for lesser characters. And there's usually a nugget of truth in such stories. Ahern was a chancer and Cowen a bluffer. And Sean FitzPatrick? Well, he ran Anglo Irish Bank . . .

But nothing is that simple. The crash – and the austerity that followed – happened in the international context of a decades-long struggle between two wings of capitalism. Although the crash had its own Irish tint, it was part of a global catastrophe that had been building for three decades. The policies that led to the Celtic Tiger were similar to policies that thrived across the globe.

And the policies that have been inflicted on us since the economy collapsed emerged from the same womb as the policies that caused the crash.

Economists are still arguing about what caused the Great

Depression of the 1930s. Eighty years from now, there will still be conflicting views on the 2008 collapse. The major political parties have broadly agreed on a cover story to explain why and how the current crisis overwhelmed them. In this chapter, using broad strokes, we'll paint an alternative view.

The 1929 stock market crash, and the Great Depression that followed, frightened the hell out of political leaders and economists. There had long been a strong belief in keeping the state's nose out of business: let the markets run the economy. That wasn't so popular any more. After the Second World War, the longing for stability led to the rise of a version of capitalism promoted by economist John Maynard Keynes. It argued that the state should regulate the market, in line with the public good.

The Keynesians and the free marketeers were in broad agreement on a lot of things, but this basic divide would continue through most of the twentieth century, and beyond. Whole schools of economics grew up around this conflict. Each side had its theories and its lauded thinkers. The free marketeers had Friedrich Hayek and Milton Friedman; the advocates of government intervention in the market had J. K. Galbraith and Paul Krugman.

The free marketeers were in later years referred to as monetarists or neoliberals. The Keynesians were said to be in favour of a 'mixed economy', except by those who saw them as dictatorial communists.

At the core of neoliberalism is a belief that the free market is the wisest, most efficient method of human organization ever developed. The market, left as free as possible, rewards the efficient and punishes the waster. Government, say the neoliberals, should be as small as possible, and 'interfere' as little as possible in the decisions of the market.

Privatize as much as possible. Private companies in search of a profit are always and everywhere more efficient than the state, they say.

Deregulate, to free from red tape the unique talents of the entrepreneur.

Cut taxes, so that the rich have the freedom to wield their wealth creatively.

Essentially, the collective will of the people is supposed to be expressed through their buying and selling, in both the consumer marketplace and on the stock exchange. And government intervention in any part of this interferes with the freedom of the market, and therefore the freedom of the people. Among the more passionate supporters of this creed, free-market capitalism is held to be the very definition of freedom. Electing a government is a secondary aspect of democracy, not much more than a technicality.

A prominent part of Keynesianism was a belief that the state had a role in providing a stimulus to the economy in times of recession, effectively creating jobs when private investors retreated from the markets out of fear of losing money.

Famously, Keynes gave an exaggerated version of how this worked in a time of mass unemployment. Suppose the Treasury officials were to fill old bottles with banknotes, he said, and bury them at suitable depths in disused coal mines. And fill up the mineshafts with town rubbish.

Then, they could leave it to private enterprise to employ workers to dig the banknotes up again. 'There need be no more unemployment . . . It would, indeed, be more sensible to build houses and the like; but if there are political and practical difficulties in the way of this, the above would be better than nothing.'

Towards the end of the Second World War, under the influence of Keynesianism, a now cautious capitalism created activist international bodies such as the World Bank and the International Monetary Fund. They were designed to step in to provide stability when the markets undermined capitalism.

Keynesianism became the new orthodoxy. And for about twenty-five years there was unprecedented stability and prosperity, during which the political pendulum swung slightly to the left. In the 1970s, inflation and stagnation became problems. And rising expectations led to prolonged industrial disputes, as capital and labour fought to increase their share of income.

As a consequence, the political pendulum swung sharply to the right. In 1979, Margaret Thatcher was elected in the UK, and Ronald Reagan in the USA the following year. Keynesianism, having failed, was discarded; free-market extremism became the new orthodoxy. Implementing the theories of intellectuals such as Hayek and Friedman, the triumphant neoliberals ensured that belief in the supremacy of the markets was even more gung-ho than before the 1929 crash.

Once more, the notion was in fashion that freedom consists largely of cutting back the state, to allow the deregulated market freely to wreak its 'creative destruction'.

In the UK, Thatcher broke the legendary miners' union and wrapped workers in a straitjacket of anti-union legislation. In the USA, Reagan did something similar with air-traffic controllers. The two leaders launched a crusade to restore the unfettered dominance of free markets – deregulating, privatizing and cutting taxes.

The overnight deregulation of the financial-services business created a blizzard of money. The bright young things of Wall Street and the City of London invented new ways to gamble, and developed new ways of building debt – with vastly greater profits, salaries and bonuses. The catch-cry of the remainder of the 1980s was the crude boast, 'loads-a-money'.

When the Soviet Union collapsed in 1990 the West declared victory in the Cold War. For decades, the stagnant authoritarian USSR had bullied workers into attempting to meet the targets set by an anti-democratic elite. The same elite bankrupted the country, economically and politically, as it tried to match the West, missile for missile, ploughing huge expenditure into the arms race.

In the West, the intellectuals deemed this collapse to be 'the end of history'. One of Ronald Reagan's advisers, Francis Fukuyama, wrote a book of that title and suggested that humanity had reached 'the end point of mankind's ideological evolution and the universalisation of Western liberal democracy as the final form of human government'.

Neither Fukuyama nor anyone else explained how the collapse of a totalitarian state with an oppressed working class validated Western capitalism – but, back then, right-wing intellectuals got a bit carried away with themselves. They and their political admirers took the collapse of Stalin's legacy as a divine endorsement of free-market extremism.

This victory was significant: it closed off any hint of debate or even thought within mainstream society about what was happening. The external enemy was defeated, his philosophy bankrupt; therefore, the victor must be on the right path.

Most people didn't think all that deeply about what was happening. Politicians offer tax cuts; people vote for them. Few outside the world of politics and economics had heard of neoliberalism. Fewer knew where it was headed. Many who followed its demands didn't call it that, they called it freedom from bureaucracy.

Neoliberal policies openly benefited the rich. The theory was: free the rich from regulation, cut their taxes, let their creativity run free. The more money they make, the better. And their excess money will 'trickle down' to the rest of us.

And, as long as there's some money trickling down, the great majority get on with their lives and don't look at the detail of what's happening.

The free market had come to be regarded by mainstream politicians, academics and the media as the pinnacle of human achievement in politics and economics. From now on, to doubt its primacy was heresy. In the UK, Labour swung into line, as the Blair regime took the Thatcher ideology as its model. In the USA, Bill Clinton found most of this agreeable.

Here, the Labour Party expressed its acceptance of the supremacy of the markets.

Externally, Soviet Communism was defeated. Internally, Keynesianism was declared redundant. In the words of one University of Chicago professor: the idea of fiscal stimulus, for instance, was taught in university courses 'only for its fallacies'. One scholar, Paul Davidson, noted in 2007: 'the teaching of Keynes's revolution in theory and policy is dead, at least in economics textbooks, the writings of mainstream economists, and speeches of governmental policy makers whether they be "liberal" or "conservative".'

The point is not that Keynesianism was beaten. It's quite likely that even without the triumph of the free-market extremists there would have been a major economic crisis. Keynesian economics hadn't prevented the crisis of the 1970s.

The point is that the free-market extremists had complete and utter dominance – economically, politically, culturally. There was no resistance, there was no debate. When problems arose, no opposing arguments had the clout seriously to dispute the principles of neoliberal free-market extremism. Those principles were held to be as sacred as any religious doctrine.

To think outside of this doctrine – well, that was unthinkable.

In the USA, many intellectuals came to believe that the financial innovations of the bankers and government manipulation of monetary policy had eliminated the age-old boom–slump cycle, in which a boom was followed by a recession. They called it the 'Great Moderation', and wrote books about it.

When politicians, economists and their media cheerleaders later said things like 'There is no alternative', and 'It's the only game in town,' they meant it. There were no possibilities existing outside the parameters set by the authoritarianism of the free markets.

(And, even now, after their theories have led to an international recession, mainstream academics, politicians and business people, steeped in the ideology of neoliberalism, seem as incapable of fresh thought as Stalin's fans after the fall of communism.)

In the USA, the Federal Reserve, under free-market absolutist Alan Greenspan, lived by these semi-religious principles. His example was widely followed. Greenspan was treated as a high priest, a striker-down of heresies.

The main character in the 1987 Hollywood movie *Wall Street*, Gordon Gekko, summed up the philosophy then gripping the global financial-services business. That philosophy said that freedom to make money, with the least possible hindrance, is the best way to achieve the greatest good:

> Greed, for lack of a better word, is good. Greed is right.
> Greed works. Greed clarifies, cuts through, and captures
> the essence of the evolutionary spirit. Greed, in all of its
> forms; greed for life, for money, for love, knowledge, has
> marked the upward surge of mankind.

That, of course, was just a movie. However, it was an accurate reflection of what was going on. The previous year, stock trader Ivan Boesky delivered the commencement address at the School of Business Administration at the University of California, Berkeley. Boesky, one of Wall Street's most successful money hunters, laid down the moral law for students:

> Greed is all right, by the way. I want you to know that.
> I think greed is healthy. You can be greedy and still feel
> good about yourself.

The business students laughed and applauded. Some of them, when the whole thing collapsed twenty years later, were surely senior bankers in Lehman Brothers, Bear Stearns, Goldman Sachs and the other monsters of finance.

Boesky was subsequently sentenced to three and a half years in jail for insider trading. He had no problem paying the accompanying fine of $100 million.

The movie character Gordon Gekko, intended as the portrayal of a villain, became a role model within the financial business. Free markets and the values they encouraged became unquestionable truths. To mainstream politicians, media commentators and academics, greed had become a valid motivator. Greed was now regarded not only as morally acceptable, but socially beneficial.

Here, the neoliberal creed achieved a kind of semi-religious status within Official Ireland. The politicians, the economists, the bankers, the entrepreneurs and their media cheerleaders couldn't articulate where the boom had come from, but they could enthuse about the dynamic of the free market, about deregulation, about privatization and about tax cuts.

They seemed to have evidence on their side: the boom existed, more people were working, there were all these shiny new buildings – only a begrudger would question this new Ireland. So, over the next few years, the Irish elite had complete dominance of the political and economic terrain. With only weak resistance from sceptics and alleged begrudgers, they reshaped the economy in their own image.

4

How Much of It was Real?

THE FIRST WOBBLE CAME in March 2007. The Irish stock exchange dropped €5 billion in one day. Which made some of us wonder if an economic earthquake was about to take the ground from under our feet.

We civilians hadn't a clue what was happening, but it sounded like maybe there was something wrong, deep in the bowels of the economy.

The experts, with nervous grins on their ashen faces, assured us the wobble was merely a 'market correction', a slight adjustment. The markets, they said, had been so wonderfully prosperous for so long that a slight 'correction' was needed. Far from being worried, they said, we should be pleased that this stabilizing mechanism had kicked in. In fact, the experts insisted, what had happened was a good thing. Whatever it was.

'Dance on,' said the politicians.

'Borrow more,' said the bankers.

'Full speed ahead,' said the property speculators.

'*Yeee haaa!*' said the media.

Only malcontents and loony lefties would dare question the expertise of the small army of super-special bankers, entrepreneurs, brokers, traders, analysts, think tankers, pet academics, 'independent' economists and regulators on whose every word the politicians and the media doted.

And, underneath us all, the economic earthquake gathered power. Eighteen months later, it tore everything apart.

At a point when something might have been done to cushion the blow, to take the edge off what was coming, the politicians and the economists and the specialist journalists were otherwise engaged.

A handful of worriers spoke up. Among them were Professor Morgan Kelly of the University College Dublin economics department, journalists George Lee and Richard Curran and showbiz economist David McWilliams. The rest of the people who should have known better became Celtic Tiger groupies, and slagged off the moaners. Some of the experts were working for the moneylenders. Others were swept along in the madness. Some had their doubts but bowed to patriotic intimidation; it was irresponsible, they were warned, to 'talk down the economy'. So, they shut up.

For some of us, the figures never added up – but most of us know damn all about economics. The elite kept repeating, for instance, that we had attracted lots of foreign investment because we had 'the best education system in the world'. And we wondered: how come so many of our kids are being educated in shanty schools, with rats in the walls and ceilings that occasionally collapse?

We had endless 'reform' of the two-tier health system, announcements of 'world-class' this and 'state-of-the-art' that. Yet the hospital queues grew longer, patients lingered and died on trolleys in corridors. If the Celtic Tiger was everything we were told it was, how come there were so many housing estates around the country with no one living in them?

How long could we go on selling houses to one another at ever increasing prices? Was this really the way to sustainable prosperity? We noted that our houses were worth five or six times what we paid for them, but this wasn't real money, was it?

If we were as rich as they said we were, how come so many people were borrowing so much money just to keep going?

And if and when the trade in overpriced houses slowed down, what would happen?

When we needed straight answers, we got cheerleading. It was as though the politicians and the bankers and their media groupies had become too frightened to contemplate the answers to such questions. They chattered about a 'soft landing' and crossed their fingers.

And when it crashed, it was as though all that prosperity had been an illusion. With bewildering speed we were hustled into a wasteland of austerity, with no real explanation of what had happened or what was going to happen.

How much of it was real? All that stuff about how we worked so hard we were 'cash rich and time poor'? In the social pages of the newspapers and magazines, couples complained that they hadn't time for sex. Remember Breakfast Roll Man? This was the stereotypical worker who grafted so hard, got to the site so early, all he had time to eat was a lump of raw cholesterol stuffed into a bap. It was like none of that ever happened.

We worked hard, all right.

Later, when it all fell apart, it was easy to see the whole Celtic Tiger thing as one massive delusion – a frolic financed on borrowed money. And it suits some people to see it that way. We sinned, our politicians and their experts tell us. We all partied, said Brian Lenihan. We went mad, said Enda Kenny. And now we must make amends, by doing penance and obediently accepting whatever austerity policies are laid down for us.

That was no frolic. We worked damned hard. From 1994 to 2000 we got some results: jobs, measurable growth – though some took a bigger share than others.

There was also a lot of bullshit pumped out, at the time, about how the Irish had finally discovered our 'inner entrepreneur'. It was the kind of thing the rich like to flatter themselves about – their unique talents, long buried and now visible to all. As one deluded banker put it: 'It was as if, overnight, we discovered just how good we were.'

At the start, it wasn't either of these things. It wasn't a borrowing spree. And it wasn't some mystical explosion of entrepreneurial savvy.

There were three distinct stages to the Celtic Tiger phenomenon. And there were tangible reasons for why each stage developed as it did. Real-world reasons. Not mumbo-jumbo.

The first stage, from 1994, was a period of genuine economic growth, propelled by a lot of things, including our hard work. But that period ended around 2000.

The second stage was a couple of years of muddling along, of uncertainty, with politicians who weren't up to the job of building on these achievements. But they had builder friends, and, hey . . .

The third stage was the Celtic Bubble, puffed up from about 2003 until it burst in 2008.

There is, of course, a fourth stage – the one we're now in; a stage of panic and cruelty, as those responsible for the debacle dump gigantic debts on to the rest of us. Here, and across Europe, we've been put through a stage of fanatical austerity that has undermined the real economy, in an extremist attempt to balance the books.

Let's look at the first stage, when there was real growth.

The figures tell the story. Economically, the 1980s were truly miserable, with high unemployment and emigration. It was 1994 before the 16 per cent unemployment rate began falling. By 1999 it was 5 per cent. Annual economic growth was averaging 8 per cent, more than double what it had been over the previous thirty years.

Why?

It was mostly about timing. First, the UK and the USA were by 1993 out of recession and beginning a global boom, making it easier for Ireland to sell into those markets. Then there was the European single market.

Since the mid-1980s, the EU had been sorting out the obstacles to creating a single market across all EU countries, first, in 1987, with the Single European Act, then with the Maastricht Treaty in 1992. The upshot was, by the beginning of 1993, EU legislation had established an EU-wide internal market, with free movement of goods, services and people.

Giant American companies wanted their share of that market. And a lot of them decided they could use Ireland. The Irish would get jobs and economic stimulus; the Americans got access to a small island inside the EU that could serve as an export base – an island where the people spoke English, labour was cheap, corporate tax was low and the government was deferential to big business.

In the five years before 1990, foreign direct investment into Ireland averaged about $100 million a year. In the first seven years after 1990, this increased tenfold, to $1.1 billion a year.

After the hopelessness of the 1980s recession, the persistent un-employment, emigration, the savage public health and education cuts, we jumped on anything that looked like a job. Part-time jobs, full-time jobs, contract work, casual jobs, offices, factories, sweat-shops, unionized, non-union, staff or freelance. We took the rate for the job, or we took minimum wage. Wherever there was work to be done, we grabbed it. Unemployment plunged, the economy grew. In 1989, Ireland was nineteenth out of twenty-four OECD countries in economic growth. By 1999, it had shot up to seventh place – an astonishing cumulative growth of 83 per cent.

A somewhat excitable Canadian professor of economics who did a study of the early Celtic Tiger triumphs wrote: 'This is a moment of history the Irish have been waiting for a thousand years.'

A bit over the top, but he meant well. Before the boom started, Irish living standards were two-thirds of those of other EU countries. There were doldrum decades in which emigration was the norm, and high unemployment, with poor services and a dread feeling that things would never be any different. By the end of the 1990s, we weren't an outstandingly rich country, we'd just reached the level of living standards other European countries had been used to.

Pretty much unnoticed at the time, a remarkable thing was happening. It would eventually have a bearing on why the government has now slashed social welfare for blind people.

The trade unions were quiet; the doctrine of 'social partnership' dominated. And there were consequences.

Over a long period, from about 1970 to the mid-1980s, Irish workers had held fast to their share of the national cake. It required vigilance and militancy, the occasional bruising battle, but it ensured that living standards were at least maintained in the face of inflation.

The share of the national cake is measured by how much goes to labour and how much to capital. Labour is rewarded for work, with wages, pensions and social security. Capital is rewarded for investment, with profits, interest, dividends and rents.

In 1987, labour's share of the national income was 52 per cent; capital's was 48 – which meant, of course, that the minority who hold capital were getting almost as much of a share as the vast majority who depend on the rewards of their labour.

By 1998, labour's share of income was down to 42 per cent and capital's share had grown to 58 per cent. As the excitable Canadian professor of economics, Pierre Fortin of Quebec University, put it: 'The share of capital income has risen to an unprecedented level.'

The overall national income had grown, but the richest were getting richer. Professor Fortin: 'The country has become an extremely profitable place to do business.' Labour remained cheap. Professor Fortin found an 'extraordinary improvement in Irish international cost competitiveness since the mid-1980s'. He wrote: 'During this period Irish unit labour costs [measured in US dollars] increased by only half as much as unit labour costs among competitors.'

The emergence of a top layer of the increasingly rich is visible in the figures. The World Top Incomes Database, hosted at the Paris School of Economics, shows only a slight increase in average Irish incomes between 1980 and 1990. The next decade was a different story.

Bottom 90 per cent of earners: average income in real 2000 Irish pounds

1980	1990	2000
£8,015	£8,815	£12,105

And the top 1 per cent of earners: average income in real 2000 Irish pounds

1980	1990	2000
£70,026	£76,312	£175,523

That is, in the 1990s boom, the great mass of wage earners had a 37 per cent increase in real income. And the top 1 per cent had a 230 per cent increase. In 1980, the average earner in the top 1 per cent was getting 8.7 times what the average of the bottom 90 per cent earned. By 2000, that had gone up to 14.5 times.

And these were just the common-or-garden high earners – those who were tax resident and fully compliant. Beyond that, there were the tax exiles and the like – and the high earners who lived here and who managed to conceal significant portions of their wealth from the Revenue Commissioners.

While 'social partnership' produced stability, and it gave the union leaders a certain status, and the leaders could point to social achievements, there was a price. Society was becoming more unequal.

Union membership was falling. It was harder to organize the increased numbers of casual and part-time workers; increasing numbers of companies were actively anti-union. At rank-and-file level, with little to do but accept the agreements negotiated by the union leaders, the sinews of the movement had atrophied. A generation of union officials hadn't ever organized a strike or a campaign of any sort and wasn't very good at recruiting. Trade-union membership in 1980 was 55 per cent of the workforce. By 1999, it was 38 per cent. By 2010, it would be 31 per cent.

As organized labour went into decline, the national ethos would be set by a growing managerial class, by the financial services, by the ever-present consultants – a self-conscious, ambitious layer of people with distinct economic interests. And, above that layer, an even thinner layer of the super-rich.

All of these had the ears of the politicians, they had the loyalty and admiration of networks of the comfortable classes. They provided the media with jubilant copy. They were idolized by the top layer of the civil service. It was the values of these layers of the exceptionally rich and their wannabe admirers that would set the national tone through the years that followed.

And those values were carried into the heart of government by a small number of politicians who found the old political ways oppressive, the old economic ways ineffective.

5

Contagion

CHARLIE HAUGHEY, AT HIS Taoiseach's desk, had finished his business with one of his senior ministers. A visitor stood just inside the doorway of Haughey's office, sent in by the secretary, the next in line for an audience with the taoiseach.

The visitor watched the minister take his leave of Haughey. 'Right so, Taoiseach,' the minister said. 'Thank you, Taoiseach.'

Haughey waved the minister away and looked up to his visitor. He gestured the visitor forward.

All the while, the minister was backing away from the taoiseach's desk, backing towards the exit, still facing the great man, his posture one of servility. 'Thank you, Taoiseach,' he repeated.

The visitor, not a member of Haughey's party, watched in fascination and repulsion.

To remain a senior member of Haughey's royal court in the 1980s, you had to be good at grovelling. By the winter of 1986, some prominent politicians had had enough. If pushed, they could mention the odd policy reason for quitting Fianna Fáil and setting up the Progressive Democrats (PDs), but that was almost an afterthought. Anyone with a strong sense of self-respect had a powerful motive for getting out from under the obnoxious, self-important and transparently corrupt little bully.

In search of policies to differentiate them, in an Ireland steeped in recession, the new party looked across the Irish Sea and across the Atlantic, to the deregulated fields of money, and were inspired. The notion of the supremacy of the markets was fiercely contagious.

At the PDs' first public meeting, in a hotel in Sutton, Mary Harney was visibly nervous. She was thirty-two, she'd never worked outside politics and she'd taken a big and brave step in quitting Fianna Fáil. That evening, the nearest she came to a statement of principles was to say that the economy was in an awful state and would get far worse unless 'somebody, somewhere does something about it'. As she sat down, there was thunderous applause.

The young Harney stirred a warm response in voters that some of the other founders, such as Dessie O'Malley and Michael McDowell, never would.

For the first forty years of independence, Ireland had been stagnant. The de Valera generation kept trying to establish an Ourselves Alone paradise. Frugal but pure, that was the theory. Materially poor, but spiritually rich. You could believe that as long as you ignored the screams from the industrial schools, the tears from the Magdalene Laundries, and the perpetual unemployment, the mass emigration and the barefoot children you could see on the streets right up to the beginning of the 1960s. And many had no trouble ignoring all of that.

By the mid-1980s, Fianna Fáil and Fine Gael smelled stale. If you weren't part of the tribe, you had trouble telling what they stood for. Labour pranced around throwing radical shapes, waiting for the opportunity to prop up Fine Gael in a coalition government. The PDs seemed fresh – they were for tax cuts, and who likes paying tax? If some of their other policies didn't seem quite worked out, maybe that would change. At their first general election, in 1987, the PDs took almost 12 per cent of the vote.

So far, they were opposed to Haughey's vulgarity and his corruption. They wanted peace in the North, believed the route to peace was to suppress the IRA. Beyond that, the success of Thatcher and Reagan had helped the PDs put some sort of shape to their policies.

They dare not publicly invoke the names of Thatcher or Reagan, but they recited versions of the policies that were seen as successful across the water. They were for the free market. And privatization. And deregulation. And, of course, there were always those tax cuts. They didn't seem to have a thorough grounding in the intellectual basis of neoliberal policies. It was as though they had heard about them at a dinner party and decided: Hey, this sounds like something we could get behind.

For a while it seemed as if they might attract one big time Fianna Fáiler to the new party: Charlie McCreevy. He seemed to have the same devotion to uninhibited markets, but McCreevy stuck with the safer route to office, Fianna Fáil.

The free-market hawks' dream team of McCreevy as Minister for Finance, with Mary Harney as Tánaiste and Minister for Enterprise, in a government headed by Bertie Ahern, eventually took the stage in June 1997. Ahern was Mr Agreeable. If it got him re-elected, he was for it. So, the era of tax cuts and light-touch regulation took off.

And everyone soon knew that it was the McCreevy tax cuts, freeing the wealth of the entrepreneurs, giving citizens the right to spend more money, that stimulated the market and got the Celtic Tiger roaring and employment soaring. As Conor Lenihan, Fianna Fáil TD, put it: 'Charlie McCreevy can claim to have played a decisive role in changing our state from one where its very financial viability was questioned to one that is now thriving.'

Now we know that, like much else, that wasn't true. It was the opposite of the truth.

Things were pretty desperate at the beginning of the 1990s. By 1993, very reluctantly, then Minister for Finance Bertie Ahern agreed to devalue the Irish pound. Exports surged. The incoming Fine Gael/Labour coalition government didn't realize a boom was under way. By the time they did, they had lost office in 1997, to Bertie Ahern and Mary Harney.

From 1994, the economy took off. Three years before the Ahern/Harney government came to power, GDP annual growth hit 5.8 per cent.

And 9.7 per cent in 1995.

And 7.7 per cent in 1996.

In 1997, before McCreevy got his feet under the table at Finance, GDP growth hit 10.7 per cent.

To see this as evidence that the 'very financial viability' of the state was threatened, you'd have to be – well, let us be kind – you'd have to be a Fianna Fáil minister.

And it was the same with employment.

In 1994, 3.2 per cent growth in employment.

In 1995, 5 per cent growth in employment.

In 1996, 3.7 per cent growth in employment.

In 1997, 3.8 per cent growth in employment.

It was at least 1999 before the McCreevy tax cuts could have had any effect on the economy. In the meantime, in 1998, the growth in employment was 8.3 per cent.

In short, the real boom predated the arrival of McCreevy and his free-market chums. They didn't create the boom, they squandered it.

Like every good little free marketeer, the Ahern/Harney government sought to keep the market free of what they saw as state interference and red tape. The policy of light-touch regulation was in place – in a country where regulation had never been terribly heavy.

In 2005, serious allegations of mistreatment of workers were laid against Gama, a Turkish multinational employing construction workers in Ireland. In the controversy that followed, the minister responsible, Mary Harney, quite rightly pointed out that there were all sorts of labour-protection laws. The legislation accorded with European standards, so the controversy wasn't the government's fault.

Here was an example of a peculiarly Irish solution to the problem of how to protect the freedom of the market. The government had to install regulatory legislation to keep the unions and the EU happy. Yet its own ideology frowned on anything that interfered with the supremacy of market forces. Answer: create the laws, but not the means to enforce them.

There was just a handful of labour inspectors. Too much work, too few people; a high turnover of staff, with long gaps when posts weren't filled. Even when the inspection staff was increased after the Gama controversy, there were just twenty-one inspectors to police legislation covering over a million and a half workers. (There were more than twice as many dog wardens.)

Much later, blame would be showered on to the heads of regulators for failing to control the banks. And it was clear that they hadn't done so. But light-touch regulation was never the choice of individual regulators, it was state policy all along.

Light-touch regulation went hand in hand with deference to the markets and a strong belief that Ireland's entrepreneurial talents were being held captive by the red tape of regulation. Leading politicians saw their task as being to liberate the 'wealth creators', so they could work their magic.

Essentially, the 'wealth creators' had the run of the country. The builders decided what would be built, and – in concert with the land hoarders – where it would be built. The shape of the economy was left to the bankers to decide. The boom had affected the culture to such an extent that it was commonly assumed there was a layer of elite movers and shakers who knew how to get things done. The politicians, the regulators and large swathes of the populace deferred to them.

6

They *Imagine*! They *Create*!

W<small>E USED TO HAVE</small> business people. These were people who spotted a need, arranged to meet that need, for a price. Goods were manufactured, distributed, retailed or a service was performed; people were employed, they spent money and that employed more people. And when someone asked what you did, you said, 'I make forklift trucks,' or furniture or wellington boots. Or you distributed them or retailed them, or you handled the accounts of a company that did. Or you fixed their machines, provided their transport or printed their labels.

This was known as being 'in business', and it was usually regarded as an honourable, useful thing to do.

Some time during the Celtic Tiger era, being in business became old-fashioned. There arose the concept of the entrepreneur – people with risk running in their veins, with minds hewn from solid blocks of ambition. You became an entrepreneur in the same way you might once have become a poet – by declaring yourself to be one.

It's useful when people get an idea and set up a structure and turn the idea into a product or a service, with a premise and a business plan and a workforce, and they build it into something that has a solid base and a future.

You could call that entrepreneurship, if it made you feel a bit more cool to use a French word. And, as the country prospered, there were lots of people who began to manufacture smoked salmon or set up a business selling yogurt made from their own recipe, people who designed clothes, built furniture or perfected a new piece of software or a new range of door handles, creating something that didn't exist before. People did these things because they wanted to make a living or they saw a gap in the market and thought they might become wealthy. They sometimes did it because they loved doing it, and there's no better work than work that satisfies.

But, alongside this, we got increasing numbers of spoofers talking about their 'vision'. Any work-shy hustler who opened a business with Daddy's money became an entrepreneur. One of the benefits of being such an entrepreneur is that you didn't actually do the work. Once you set up the business you moved on to your next vision, while taking an income from the profits.

Entrepreneurship became mostly about two things (apart from wearing sunglasses indoors): you had to come up with business ideas (usually by going to the USA for a couple of months and keeping your eyes open); and you had to get a bank to lend you money. As time went by, getting a loan from an Irish bank meant you had to meet their strict borrowing criteria: you had to have a pulse.

So, you had people in business: people who started projects, people who worked for them, suppliers to that project, customers, etc. – otherwise known as the real economy. And you had an amount of froth on the top of the economy, people who fancied themselves as 'risk takers' and 'wealth creators'.

By and by, you had adverts like this playing incessantly on the radio:

In business, everything starts with the Entrepreneur.
They imagine! They create!
They fan the sparks of imagination, turning ideas into reality!
In short – they make it happen.
If you'd like to salute and reward one of these unique
        individuals . . .

And so on. It was almost as though a new subspecies of the human race had evolved.

The Ernst & Young radio advert for its Entrepreneur of the Year Award became part of the soundtrack of Celtic Tiger Ireland. The culture of ambition was in the air. Daily, the radio presented business reports in which executives gave versions of their own success which were usually unchallenged. The newspapers broadened their business coverage; sometimes useful, often flattering.

Nothing wrong with interviewing these people – they had a story to tell. But the work was seldom done that allowed the interviewer to dispute the stories they offered. Or to analyse what was happening overall within the economy. The treadmill of news ensured that there was always a new CEO to interview, a new set of results over which the interviewer and the CEO could purr.

(There was an exception to this. George Lee, the RTÉ economics editor, persisted in looking beneath the surface figures, displaying an awareness of the big picture. This led to Lee being mocked as a doom monger by the cheerleaders of the Celtic Bubble. He didn't just report what was said, he analysed it, his point of departure being whether this was good for the citizens. Sadly, just when we most needed him, Lee strayed into Fine Gael, for whom he won a by-election and became a trophy TD. After eight months he abruptly quit. His sceptical analysis has never been replaced within RTÉ.)

As the free-market culture threw up increasing numbers of millionaires, the gossip pages were full of the antics of celebrity entrepreneurs. RTÉ television broadcast the Entrepreneur of the Year Award – and it was dreadfully dull viewing. Inevitably, television sexed things up and gave us the likes of *The Apprentice* and *Dragons' Den*, cartoon versions of business techniques in which hopefuls played out their dreams for our entertainment. It seemed like every channel had its own property show, urging us to buy, to decorate and to sell one house, so we could buy, decorate and sell a bigger house.

Culturally, the cult of the supremacy of the markets was all over the place: gloating company executives on morning radio; brash fantasists in television's business game shows in the evening, stabbing one another in the back.

From the beginning, the politicians were in love with the notion of creating what they called 'an enterprise culture'. They decided it would be peachy if hundreds of thousands of us bought shares and simpered as we watched our share portfolios grow.

To get things off to a flying start, they chose the state's telecoms company, Telecom Éireann. The European Union was saturated in fashionable neoliberalism principles, and EU rules decreed that Telecom must be privatized by 2003. The Fianna Fáil/Progressive Democrat government, elected in 1997, decided they couldn't wait that long. By 1999, it was ready to float Telecom on the market. They spent several million pounds changing the company's name to Eircom. Parts of it were then sold off and – in July 1999 – Eircom shares went on sale.

The state got about £5 billion from the sale, which it prudently put into the National Pension Reserve Fund, to ensure there would be a sufficient nest egg for future pensions. (There the money sat, as the fund grew over the next decade. Until the banks collapsed. At which point the government drained the NPRF's reserves, handing the money over to the bankers.)

Meanwhile, a lot of people made a lot of money out of the

privatization of Eircom. Various consultants, advisers and lawyers got fees totalling about £70 million. The employees got a share of the takings. And, at management levels, everyone seemed to be on rock-star wages.

An aggressive marketing campaign left citizens in no doubt that only fools would fail to bet on this sure thing. It was easy money, like getting a look at Saturday's winning Lotto numbers on Friday night. People plundered their life's savings to buy shares. Others got phone calls from their banks, offering loans so they could gamble.

A total of 570,000 people bought into the easy-money culture. 'Hold on to your shares,' said the experts, as the price soared from 3.90p to 5.20p. 'Two reasons to hold on to the shares, folks – first, you'll get a bonus. Second, this baby's gonna go through the roof and you'll need a wheelbarrow to collect all the folding green.'

And nine-tenths of the punters held on to their shares. And ended up stunned, disbelieving, as they quickly lost a third of the money they had invested.

The reason for the whole privatizing experiment had nothing to do with telecommunications. It had nothing to do with securing investment for the company or improving its service. It wasn't even about encouraging competition, which was the ostensible reason for the EU privatization policy. It was all about getting people into the habit of buying shares.

Why?

Because everyone knew that The Market was the sun that casts its kindly light upon us as we basked in its bountiful rays. The whole Eircom disaster had nothing to do with business, it was about two things: passing a profitable, useful business into private hands; and trying to turn us into a share-owning, market-centred society.

And the disaster had only begun.

As a state-owned company, Eircom had been efficient and profitable, with 13,000 workers and a bright future. It was supposed to have a crucial role in providing infrastructure for the brave new online world into which we were all moving. Privatized, a plaything for the rich, it became a debt-ridden hulk.

The limping company was taken over by a consortium of venture capitalists led by Tony O'Reilly. The function of venture capitalists is to make profit. At each stage, the venture capitalists made millions. At each stage, Eircom was loaded with debt.

Eircom was worth, in today's money, €8.4 billion at the time of its privatization, and was debt free. By early 2012, it was on its way into examinership, with net debts of almost €4 billion. By then, it had shed all but 5,500 of its 13,000 jobs.

Since venture capitalists typically aren't primarily concerned with a company's long-term interests, they have little incentive to invest for long-term development. And Eircom needed huge investment if it was to provide the broadband infrastructure the country needed. The company stagnated in debt, the country lagged behind in broadband.

But the culture of inequality that was being encouraged was too strong to be reversed by even the Eircom disaster. The notion of huge rewards for special people received a big boost as the Eircom drama played out.

Eircom's chief executive, Alfie Kane, became something of a role model for the Celtic Tiger culture.

Alfie's basic salary was £300,000 – a lot of money now, and even more so thirteen years ago. On top of this, Alfie split £1.2 million in bonuses with another manager. It was a reward for 'getting the company into a healthy state before privatization'.

But wasn't that his job, for which he got a hefty salary? Just what is it that Alfie wouldn't do for a mere £300,000 that he'd feel 'incentivized' to do by having his pockets stuffed with larger chunks of cash?

When Alfie resigned in 2002, the price of Eircom shares had

halved, the company showed a £47 million loss to March of that year. Total company earnings were down 22 per cent, operating profit down 38 per cent. And Alfie's salary was now £444,000.

Alfie got £1.08 million compensation for loss of office, with another £2.8 million into his pension pot.

Mr Kane wasn't the first Irish chief executive to get rock-star wages, and he certainly wouldn't be the last. The Eircom privatization was supposed to be a showcase of the 'enterprise culture'. And it was. But perhaps not in the way that the politicians hoped.

So, by the year 2000, when the New Gentry were bidding at the charity auction in Limerick, the values of the markets had long taken root.

And, we had the cult of the entrepreneur.

A tax base that was being steadily undermined.

A government that saw regulation as an interference with freedom.

Interest rates set low, by the European Central Bank, to suit the larger EU countries.

Now, if only we had a property bubble . . .

7

Republican Days

T HERE WERE PEOPLE IN the room who looked like they'd come straight from the set of *The Sopranos*. Big men in tight-fitting suits, some of them smoking broom-handle cigars. It was the last week of March 2002, in the downstairs bar in Buswell's Hotel, across the road from Leinster House. The pints and the shorts were flowing; there was an air of celebration. There were a few media people around, but mostly it was Fianna Fáil members and hangers-on, and guests. And you could feel the sense of fellowship. It wasn't exactly the Galway Tent, but it was a fund-raising shindig.

The previous year, foot-and-mouth restrictions forced the party to cancel various events at which their fans could give them money. So someone came up with a plan: produce a book based on the party archives, and sell it.

It was titled *Republican Days* and it cost £38 in bookshops. Here at the launch, you could buy it for £30.

The book was handsomely produced, but it wasn't a great addition to anyone's library. It had some mildly interesting photos of old Fianna Fáil election posters. For the most part, though, the 'archives' consisted of the kind of trivia for which paper shredders were invented. It had thirty-year-old letters from sad individuals with too much time on their hands, asking for permission to set up a Fianna Fáil cumann. And pages and pages of reproductions of handwritten letters that rambled aimlessly. In case any reader mistook these missives for something worth reading, the caption beside a reproduction of some of those letters announced that they 'ramble aimlessly'. And those particular letters were, for some reason, reproduced twice. In colour.

In short, the book was a bore. But that didn't matter. The faithful would buy it – and the country then was full of true believers. Sales of the book would bring in a fair whack – but the real money was in the advertisements inside the book.

In fact, the adverts were what the book was all about. They told you far more about the Fianna Fáil of 2002 than anything the text of the book told you about the history of the party.

No fewer than twelve adverts were for bars and hotels.

And eight adverts for people who sold cars and trucks.

A couple featured solicitors.

A firm of accountants.

And forty-five adverts for builders and developers.

There was just something about the building and developing business that compelled its movers and shakers to throw money at Fianna Fáil. When the party rang the money bell, sheer devotion to the democratic process kicked in and the builders and developers reached for their wallets.

From way back, builders and developers were fond of Fianna Fáil, and by now they had the thickest wallets – passing out the meat business, which used to be a reliable source of funding for the political parties. By the 1980s, the relationship between developers and Fianna Fáil was so well established that it must have seemed to some that bunging the party was as much a part of a development as assembling the site.

Consider Frank Dunlop, who moved from party booster to briber-in-chief, to developer.

Frank was first a Fianna Fáil press officer, helping the media see how wonderful the party was. In that role, he became familiar to politicians at all levels of the party. He later turned up at council meetings, watching councillors vote through permission for development deals. His role was to represent a developer, and if politicians needed a donation to help them realize the proper thing to do in the interests of their constituents, Frank had a plentiful supply of brown envelopes stuffed with convincing documents.

With admirable devotion to multitasking, Frank also had a financial interest in some developments. When one project didn't go through, he shrugged and told a reporter, 'I have balls of iron and a spine of steel. If we can't make a shilling here, we'll make it someplace else.' It was the maxim by which the Irish developer class operated. If they'd put it to music, it could have been the national anthem of Celtic Tiger Ireland.

The boom in the real economy slowed down around 2000, and went into neutral over the next couple of years. Internationally, around the same time, the bursting of the dotcom bubble, followed by 9/11, left the global economy in trouble. Here, the economy slowed but things were still relatively prosperous.

In 2000, the state-funded think tank, the Economic and Social Research Institute (ESRI), issued a warning. The government's plans to stoke the economy involved tax cuts and boosts for the building industry. Pouring money into construction when prices were high and the economy was still on a high was a bad move, said the ESRI. Wait a couple of years, they suggested, and when the economy needs a boost, that's the time. The tax cuts could endanger the economy in the medium term.

Such policies are called counter-cyclical. They're a standard tool of economics. When things are slow, add fuel; when the economy is hot, cool it down.

McCreevy and Harney, however, were wedded to tax cuts as part of the theology of neoliberalism. Tax cuts help free the market, therefore they are good. Ahern loved tax cuts because voters love tax cuts, and he wanted voters to love him and keep on voting for him. And they did.

The trade-union leaders loved tax cuts. Negotiating such cuts made them feel they were 'partners' with government. It improved their members' take-home pay, without having to engage in any of that yucky militancy on which people like James Connolly and James Larkin built the trade-union movement.

Employers loved tax cuts. It meant they escaped having to raise wages.

The link between Fianna Fáil and developers made a big push on construction an obvious move. Besides, the grateful developers could be relied on to keep pumping funds into the party.

The government was also working hard to get Irish emigrants to return to Ireland. Ahern would be the taoiseach to bring home the Irish diaspora. Anyway, the government needed someone to buy all those houses the developers were about to build. Answering the call from home, countless thousands of emigrants who had done well abroad sold up their homes, quit their jobs, came back to Éireann and locked themselves into decades-long, over-priced mortgages.

Here's RTÉ's economics correspondent George Lee reporting in 2000 on the government's response to the ESRI warning:

> The government has been very quick to dump on the
> ESRI advice. Finance Minister Charlie McCreevy says
> he's not particularly worried about what they said. And
> that it's a sign of our economic manhood, when we see

people wanting to come back to this country to take up
jobs. Tánaiste Mary Harney also lashed out. She insisted
the tax cuts will keep inflation down. And that people are
entitled to expect low tax rates when times are good.

With a firm grip on his economic manhood, McCreevy cut taxes
again and again and again.

We were now in the Eurozone, and interest rates were set to suit
the economy of the EU's largest countries. If the Irish government
had control of its own interest rates, some say, it would have raised
them to cool the economy. That's probably not true. There was no
sense of planning, no sense of this being a moment in time, with
connections to the past and with an influence on the future. We
were tigers, we had seized the moment, we were special. We made
our own reality.

So, borrowing was cheap.

Property speculators had their choice of tax break.

You turned on your radio and the chances were you'd hear an
economist who worked for a bank telling you not to worry, house
prices were low, the economy was fine.

We all like to think that the government – whatever we think
of its policies – is working from solid information, painstakingly
gathered by dispassionate public servants, discussed at great length,
resulting in carefully worked-out policies. We might disagree with
what the government decides, but we accept it is working from the
best possible information, and that it knows far more about these
things than the rest of us.

How, then, do we account for this?

At one stage, late in 2001, the boom well and truly over,
with public unease growing along with the job losses, Tánaiste
Mary Harney went on the RTÉ News and announced that the
'fundamentals' of the economy 'are sound'. There was a downturn

in the USA, she told us, and that was having an effect here. But, she said, the average length of a downturn in the US economy, based on historical figures, was seven months. And the USA, she said, was already five months into this downturn, so . . .

This was encouraging. Within a couple of months we'd be on the up again.

However, some hours earlier, an economist who worked for a bank had been on RTÉ's *Morning Ireland*. There was a downturn in the USA, he told us, and that was having an effect here. But, he said, the average length of a downturn in the US economy, based on historical figures, was seven months. And the USA, he said, was already five months into this downturn, so . . .

Those of us who heard both broadcasts suspected that the second-in-command of the Irish economy was picking up her info from the radio.

Through 2003 and into 2004, the property speculators – who had already stoked a property boom – went into a new, more aggressive phase. Tough hustlers who in the 1980s built an estate here, a few bungalows there, were by now putting together massive deals, building hotels, car parks and trophy office blocks, as well as throwing up housing estates on all sides.

Now, there was little connection with what was needed and what was built. One sentence from Kieran Allen's book *The Corporate Takeover of Ireland* sums up the madness. 'Between 2000 and 2004, an extra 987 hotels were built with a tax subsidy of €196 million.'

You could always hire a tame economist to explain how this gambling was based on market trends, demographics or anticipated demand. In truth, tax breaks decided what got built. As did who owned what piece of land, and where. And it depended on which bank would fund which gambler throwing up whatever seemed likely to sell quickly. And it depended on who could get which piece of land re-zoned.

Then, since brown envelopes were part of all this, and some politicians didn't see why they shouldn't get a cut of the proceeds, the free market was raging all over the place. Not so much a Celtic Tiger as a rabid wolf.

The rich and the wannabe rich could smell the money flowing back through the system. The statistics were better than ever. In July 2004, one economist made the case for stoking the overheated economy. *'Vroom-vroom!'* he assured an *Irish Times* reporter. 'The Tiger's back, *vroom-vroom!'*

So, we had a set of values influenced by the New Gentry.

We had the cult of the entrepreneur.

Politicians who saw the tax base as something that needed shrinking – and who always had one ear cocked to advice from bankers and their economists.

A government madly in love with the notion of light-touch regulation.

Interest rates set low to suit the larger countries.

And property developers pawing the ground with excitement.

Now, if only we had a banking sector that had grown used to playing fast and loose with the rules . . .

8

The Wild West

$\mathbf{B}$ACK IN FEBRUARY 1998, Siobhan Creaton revealed, in the *Irish Times*, that the country was awash with non-resident companies.

It was easy, in those days, to get confused by the term 'non-resident'. If you had fraud on your mind, there were two principal non-resident scams you could use. One was the non-resident company, the other was the bogus non-resident bank account. These should not be confused with the old-fashioned offshore account wherein you hid the money you had concealed from Revenue and/or taken in bribes.

Irish banks may be bugger all use at banking, but they've been a fountain of creativity when it comes to bending the rules.

First, the flood of non-resident companies.

A decade earlier, the British had cleaned some of the dodgier elements out of their financial-services business. As a result, a lot of people across the globe were in search of an offshore haven in which to launder their funny money. They could always go to the Cayman Islands, but that was a lot of hassle – and when people heard the word 'Cayman' they wondered if you might be a dodgy character, with something to hide.

Happily, the Irish Financial Services Centre was now up and running, heavily supported with tax breaks. Word went around. Soon, there were 40,000 non-resident companies here. Public servants with a sense of propriety were uneasy about what was going on. Others lobbied to keep things as they were.

For a column in the *Sunday Independent*, in March 1999, I did a trawl of internet sites advertising Ireland's offshore delights. The article was titled 'Welcome to Dodge City' and the adverts gave a glimpse of how this country was being portrayed abroad. Repeatedly, adverts pointed out that Ireland was 'the only full member of the EU offering these facilities'. You not only kept your money manoeuvres quiet, but you were operating from within the EU, not some little island in the sun associated in the public mind with the nudge-nudge-wink-wink wing of international finance.

The adverts emphasized that in Ireland the non-resident company would 'have the status and respectability attaching to an Irish company and will not evoke in the minds of persons dealing with it reservations which might occur in respect of companies incorporated in tax haven countries'.

In effect, you could hire this country's respectability. As one advert put it, 'Ireland is now widely considered to be one of the most sophisticated jurisdictions to operate offshore entities due to its respectable image.'

Some adverts pointed to an added attraction for those who wished to set up companies without operating anonymously. Under the Business Naturalization Scheme – since scrapped – you could effectively buy an Irish passport. If you invested a substantial amount, creating jobs, you not only got an eager workforce and low taxes, to sweeten the deal you also got an Irish passport – and that might solve all sorts of problems for you. As the adverts put it:

'Prestigious Irish nationality can be acquired under the Business Naturalization Scheme.'

One might take a moment to ponder the kind of money attracted to such a country. No doubt there were legitimate companies that took advantage of the set-up. But if you were a Moscow mafioso with money to launder, or an American executive in search of a loophole to avoid taxes back home, your thoughts might have drifted to the land of leprechauns and light-touch regulation. If you were a speculative entrepreneur who didn't want to worry about the kind of red tape that some jurisdictions use to protect their economy – come on down, the price is right.

In April 2005, *The New York Times* remarked on the 'light hand' of corporate regulation that made Dublin 'the Wild West of European finance'.

Politicians and their cheerleaders dismissed such comments. The outsiders, they implied, were merely envious of our economic manhood. Come on – haven't you heard about our awesome entrepreneurs? They *imagine*! They *create*!

What did we get out of it? Well, lawyers and accountants were reckoned to be raking in €60 million a year, servicing the non-resident crowd.

After Siobhan Creaton's article, the public servants who were unhappy with this carry-on could argue that short-term gains for the few might result in greater damage for the many. And some of the worst aspects of the non-resident scams were cleaned up – by which time many a pillar of Irish society had made a small fortune.

Ireland's banking industry had long had a creative attitude towards the law – not to mention a resourceful approach to principle, morality, truth, justice and all those other nice words they use when they're patting one another on their well-upholstered backs.

A long record of questionable behaviour prepared the ground for the lunacy that would bring the country to its knees. From the Gallagher scandal of 1990 to the systemic overcharging of customers during the boom years, the message was clear: the banks felt free to try anything that would increase profits – and if they were caught, what the hell, it wasn't like anyone was going to hold them to account.

The Gallagher scandal showed everyone that a wealthy thief could operate in this country freely and with impunity. Patrick Gallagher was a company director from the age of twelve and became another of the many graduates of Clongowes private school who left his mark on this country. He inherited a family business, then blew it on speculative development. He was not just a crook, he was an inept one. He used a bank he controlled – Merchant Banking Ltd – as though it was his own personal piggy bank. Around six hundred people, mostly small depositors, many of them elderly, lost their life savings to his criminal activities. Gallagher made the mistake of doing something similar in Northern Ireland. He was arrested there, charged, tried and sentenced to two years.

In the sainted Republic, however, the legal system was impotent. He had committed similar crimes on both sides of the border, but in the South he walked the streets a free man, feted by his peers. As Gallagher's victims faced their final years in poverty, the police, lawyers and legislators stood around scratching their arses. The thief later became something of a celebrity, boasting of how he used to bankroll another thief, Charlie Haughey.

Throughout the 1980s, as the economy worsened, people were hit with harsher taxes. Years earlier, the PAYE sector staged large protests against the unfairness of the tax system, and had been told by economists that there was 'no pot of gold'. The experts, not for the last time, got their figures wrong.

It was common knowledge that there was immense tax fraud going on within business and the professions. Some of the country's leading lights – people who lectured the rest of us on our social responsibilities – were up to their necks in it. The state arranged several tax amnesties, offering fraudsters various incentives to pay at least a portion of their taxes.

A 1988 amnesty, which was expected to bring in up to £100 million, collected over half a billion. A 1993 amnesty had a novel twist. You could go to the Revenue and confess that you had swindled the state. You had to tell them how much you'd stolen. Then you gave them just 15 per cent of that total, and you were free and clear – you no longer had any need to hide your wealth.

In short, for a 15 per cent cut, the Revenue gave you clean money.

The state pulled in about £240 million. If that was 15 per cent of the total, the crooks had been hiding about £1.6 billion they had stolen from the state. The whole thing was cloaked in confidentiality clauses, but the total was probably closer to £1.25 billion (due to varying rates paid under different parts of the amnesty). This means that about a billion in money stolen by fraud was legitimized by the state.

Meanwhile, with astonishing thoroughness, tens of thousands of people, from the comfortably off to the grossly wealthy, had opted out of the taxation system. Doctors, hoteliers, publicans, lawyers, builders, company directors, all the hordes who had salted away untaxed income, found refuge in advice from their bankers, lawyers and accountants.

If you were very wealthy, you were offered an offshore scheme. There were lots of them about. The infamous Ansbacher fraud, run by Charlie Haughey's crooked accountant Des Traynor, was one of the few secrets that eventually came to light. You gave your money to a bagman, who placed it in an offshore account. This was matched with an account in Ireland, in what was called a 'back-to-back' arrangement.

The money was technically offshore, so the Revenue couldn't

touch it. But you could withdraw what you needed from the matching back-to-back account in Ireland.

If you were important enough, you might meet the bagman in one of the Doyle hotels (founder P. V. Doyle was an Ansbacher tax evader) and be slipped a bag of cash.

For the merely well off, there were bogus non-resident accounts – thousands of them. Anyone with a bank account had to pay Deposit Interest Retention Tax (DIRT) – but not if they lived outside the state. So, you brought your money to your local bank branch and lodged it. You gave a phoney name and supplied them with a foreign address. That way, the account was non-resident and you escaped paying DIRT on the interest.

More often than not, the money lodged was hot money, concealed from Revenue and untaxed. The existence of a range of frauds was known at all levels – political, banking, Revenue, Central Bank. At one stage, Revenue worked out that there was about €4 billion in non-resident accounts. And that a high proportion of those were bogus accounts.

Later, an Oireachtas Committee investigated the bogus non-resident accounts. One of the investigators, Denis Foley TD, had his own secret Ansbacher fraud going on. When he was caught, he paid the Revenue €580,000 and the case was closed. His punishment from the Dáil was a fourteen-day suspension. He later retired on a pension of €52,956.

Of the DIRT frauds that were discovered, Revenue clawed back €1.6 billion from the fraudsters. This was on top of the amnesty money. It's known that billions of pounds were hidden in frauds – and there are threads of evidence that suggest that only a fraction of the frauds was uncovered.

These were not impulse crimes, nor were they crimes of need. They were complex frauds, carefully organized, and committed by people who were well off. They were often committed with the assistance of professionals who knew exactly which laws they were breaking. The term 'organized crime' has never been more appropriate.

Yet none of the organizers went to jail. None of the collaborators, none of the concealers. One entrepreneur created a €1.6 million fraud and was caught, charged and tried. He was fined €1,750. That is, 0.1 per cent of the loot.

Compare that with a case in which someone was convicted of writing forged cheques to the value of €5,300. They got eighteen months in jail. As the Committee of Public Accounts remarked somewhat dryly in 2005: 'This could be viewed as a glaring prejudice on the part of the establishment.'

Much later, we would hear a lot about the notion of 'moral hazard'. This means that when people do wrong or make bad choices, they have to pay a price – it has to be made clear to all that there are consequences to risk. Or else people will again and again behave recklessly, in the knowledge that they are not risking punishment.

And, when that happens, recklessness becomes the norm.

What the Irish banks, and their treasured wealthy customers, learned from a long period of persistent criminality was that there were no serious consequences for them, whatever they did. There was no moral hazard.

There were, of course, consequences for others.

The tax-evasion schemes were at their height in the 1980s and early 1990s, a period in which the state finances were in a mess. The government was spending more than it was taking in taxes. Then, as now, there was much talk about the deficit. Taxes were already high; raising them wasn't on. So, the government cut brutishly. In the mid-1980s, under a Fine Gael/Labour government, 704 acute hospital beds were closed – these were frontline services for the most serious illnesses. Another 281 second-line beds were closed – a total of 985.

The Fianna Fáil leader, Charlie Haughey, expressed outrage. He turned up at an election meeting brandishing newspaper cuttings detailing the health cuts. He had billboards around the country plastered with giant posters declaring: 'Health Cuts Hurt the Old, the Sick and the Handicapped – There is a Better Way.' He won the election.

There was indeed a better way.

The state could have collected the hundreds of millions it was owed in taxes – and which politicians, central bankers and Revenue knew was being stolen. Since Haughey himself was one of the fraudsters, and since the fraudsters were represented at all levels of the business, banking and political worlds, that was never going to happen. Instead, the health cuts deepened cruelly. Instead of 985 bed closures, Haughey closed 6,377 beds, more than half of them acute beds required for the seriously ill.

This period of cutting spending entered the mythology of the comfortable classes. They wrote some things out of history: the EU development funds (about £23 billion net, between 1973 and 2000), the surge in US investment, the 1993 devaluation of the Irish pound. They concluded that cutting state spending was the root of all growth – this fitted in with the politics of the neoliberal cult – and it justified their assault on the low- and medium-paid, the unemployed, the sick, the handicapped and schoolkids. The neoliberals even had a name for all this: 'expansionary fiscal contraction'.

The Irish politicians congratulated themselves on the 'tough decisions' they made, to 'turn the economy around'. Not only were a range of economic developments written out of history, so were the people who lingered in pain, untreated as hospital waiting lists grew. And the people who died waiting for an operation that never came.

The era of 'tough decisions' was one in which the tax fraudsters, and their accomplices in the banks and in the professions, were protected.

So, when we entered the terminal phase of the Celtic Tiger we were equipped with the lessons about how 'tough decisions' in the past had won the day.

We idolized the notion of entrepreneurship.

We had a set of values mimicking those of the New Gentry.

A tax base that was being steadily undermined.

A government with a religious devotion to light-touch regulation.

More property speculators than ever pawing the ground.

Banks with a history of bending rules, whatever worked to enlarge profits.

Bankers aware that they could act recklessly or approach the law creatively, for great gain, and they would most likely remain immune.

What could possibly go wrong?

9

When is a Bank Not a Bank?

T O MOST OF US, for most of our lives, banks were places that
kept our money safe, storing it when we were paid and giving it
out when bills were due – and if we had any money to put by, it went
into the bank or credit-union account. Banks gave us a mortgage
or a loan, and you couldn't get even a small loan without signing
lots of forms, revealing all your financial details and persuading the
bankers you could pay back the loan, no matter what happened.

Banks were considered conservative, stick-in-the-mud institutions, run by dull people with a strong aversion to risk.

Retail banks are a utility. Their raw material is money and it
flows through the economic system. Besides handling our income
and expenditure, they use the accumulated capital to underwrite
credit needed for the day-to-day running of businesses. Bank loans
allow businesses to expand and hire and pay wages. To a modern
society, the banking system is a utility as necessary as the water
pipes and electricity lines. The state imposed all sorts of regulations and requirements to ensure a balance between deposits and

investments. The state insisted on absolute obedience of rules that ensured the banks would remain solvent.

But, in recent years, many banks have no longer been just banks. They've become gambling companies, their business as much a game of chance as the businesses of Paddy Power or Ladbrookes. But on a much, much bigger scale.

In the USA, formal divisions between retail and investment banking were put in place after the Great Depression of the 1930s; by the end of 1999, these had been removed. Globally, the finance business moved into a period of frenzy, as the free-market extremists won all the arguments – economic, political, cultural – and barriers to a massive gambling spree were removed.

Gradually, in the financial centres in London and New York, then further afield, 'red tape' was cut, 'bureaucrats' were sedated or removed – the power of the markets was unleashed. New 'financial products' were dreamed up. Derivatives, credit-default swaps, securitization, collateralized debt obligations. New technology increased the speed of transactions. At the bidding of the bankers, the regulation that had kept the system stable for decades was dispensed with.

With no hint that the public should have any say in this, a system of mega-gambling had been created around the banks.

Many in the money business had only the barest notion of how these 'financial products' worked, but they didn't need to know. All they needed to do was hire energetic young hustlers and give them big bonuses for selling as much of this rubbish as they could shift. The fact that such gambling was extremely risky was ignored. After all, the gamblers held hostage the entirety of the banking system, retail and investment – and since the state implicitly guaranteed the ordinary bank depositors it could be made to guarantee anything the bankers got up to.

And the bankers got up to a lot – their bonuses depended

on results, and results depended on risk, so, globally, they went wild.

Most of us still had quaint old notions of how capitalist investment works. The TV show *Dragons' Den* is a cartoon version of that old investment model – one in which capitalists assemble spare capital, savings, profits, loans. They spot a likely invention or a niche service, perhaps some new product such as Facebook – then they invest. That way, the spare capital doesn't just lie around in a bank, it supports innovation and generates further profits for those who take the risk of investing.

The global explosion in finance services went far beyond all that. Lehman Brothers, Bear Stearns, Goldman Sachs, J. P. Morgan and the like engaged in massive high-risk behaviour. However complex the deals became, they eventually came down to betting that the price of something would go up or down. And that the price of something else would go up in one market and down in another. And, if you're fast enough to spot these movements, you can be into and out of the market before anyone has noticed the difference, pocketing big profits.

When financier Dermot Desmond was a young, successful market player, he spoke to author Ivor Kenny of the satisfaction he got from his work. The fuddy-duddy traditional firms had been less than helpful to his up-and-coming outfit. He said: 'Every pound we generate is being taken from somebody. There is satisfaction in that.' He spoke of the need to 'be caring about the community, your social responsibility' and 'the development of your country', but he had no illusions about the money business. Desmond's view of the financial services was blunt: 'The financial services are, in a sense, parasitical.'

By the beginning of the twenty-first century, this description was more appropriate than ever. The finance business sat atop the real economy, gambling on and feeding off movements in currency, commodities and shares, taking vast profits from the activities of others. Its profits and its destructive powers greatly exceed any social value it allegedly has.

Today's technology takes human judgement out of many gambles, and leaves the job to computers plugged into the markets. The biggest traders have exclusive software that enables the computer to spot market differences and act on them faster than the human mind can. Automated investment systems, guided by algorithms and triggered by market changes, automatically carry out trade in commodities, currency, shares. Anything can be bought and sold in fractions of a second, making huge profits.

In August 2012, a computer glitch in a US financial corporation, Knight Capital, caused trading in about 140 stocks to go berserk. Stocks that ordinarily traded about 100,000 times a day had within minutes been traded 4 million times, racking up billions of dollars in sales. Stock prices soared and plunged without logic. Before Knight could close things down, they'd lost $440 million. Uneasy traders remembered the infamous 'flash crash' of 2010, when $1 trillion in market value disappeared within minutes – and no one really understood how or why.

Now, people have a right to gamble. And, if that affects currency or commodity prices, and thus affects how the rest of us live – well, it's cruel and indecent and unfair, but most people don't seem to care. They buy into the free-market extremism. However, the finance business is not just an exotic form of bingo.

By the new century, in the wake of the neoliberal revolution and the explosion of the finance business, these parasitical gambling circles were embedded within the retail banking system. The risks they were taking, motivated by the bankers' desires for maximum bonuses, were silently undermining the stability of the wider economy.

In Ireland, the bankers were relatively unsophisticated. In Professor Morgan Kelly's memorable phrase, there were a number of 'faintly dim former rugby players' at the helm. They didn't much go for the complex new financial products that were all the rage on Wall Street; they preferred the old-fashioned property bubble.

As elsewhere, in Ireland the politicians found common cause with the bankers. The banks imported huge tranches of borrowed money, to lend on to builders and speculators, who built houses, estates, hotels, car parks, offices.

The politicians kept the regulation light, they re-zoned like mad, they created tax breaks – all stoking the bubble.

Already loaning money to the builders, the banks then loaned more of that borrowed money to the homebuyers and companies who bought the homes and commercial buildings.

The value of houses spiralled: that house you bought for €75,000 was now worth €300,000, then €400,000. Pretty soon it was worth almost half a million.

Soon, an unremarkable three-bedroom home in a lacklustre Dublin suburb was selling for around the same price as a house with a swimming pool in the south of France.

And, there needed be no end to this – as long as the price of property kept going up.

Which, of course, it could not do indefinitely.

A lot of people felt rich; they re-elected the politicians who made them feel that way: Fianna Fáil and the PDs.

Fine Gael and Labour pleaded for a turn in government, on the basis that they'd do more or less the same as the FF/PD shower, but more efficiently. They took issue with this and that, but they had no problem with the basic model.

And all of them – politicians, bankers, along with their tame economists and pet academics – seemed happy that the stability of the economy should be put on hazard so that a relatively small number of gamblers should get to exercise their greed.

Mind you, the state had wisely set up some sentinels who would guard the interests of the citizens. They were called regulators.

10

How Regulation Works

To THRIVE, A FINANCIAL sector in any country has to have all the right forms, in the right order, with all the boxes ticked, to reassure investors, customers and other companies that everything is above board. You have to fill in forms, get them stamped and verified and filed in triplicate in neat offices in expensive buildings. You need to be able to point towards other expensive offices to show that all this activity is being policed by hawk-eyed corporate enforcers. You need credible regulation.

And so it was in Dublin. The International Financial Services Centre (IFSC) was set up in Dublin under Charlie Haughey in 1987 as a low-tax enclave that would siphon off some of the booming financial-services business unleashed by deregulation. The initial planners of the IFSC, according to a book by two of those involved, Ray McSharry and Padraic White, were 'adamant that the Irish centre would have the highest standards of prudential supervision under the Central Bank and would strive for a reputation of the highest integrity'.

It was, at the same time, made clear to incoming financial firms that 'if they met administrative obstacles, these would be over-come'. The balancing act by the regulators can be read between the lines of the sentences that follow: 'The Central Bank and the Revenue Commissioners managed to convey not only a commit-ment to tough standards of regulation but also a strong sense of commitment to the success of the financial centre project. While doing their regulatory duty, they were also part of the Irish team.'

Laying the groundwork for the IFSC, Haughey wined and dined for Ireland, flattering the global wealthy, inviting them to see the potential of the low-tax enclave. When the president of Mitsubishi Trust arrived at Dublin airport he found that Haughey's office had arranged a police motorcycle escort.

Such brown-nosing wasn't really necessary. Mitsubishi's manag-ing director, Tadashi Kohno, was admirably frank: 'We have always been on the lookout for places with as little regulation as possible.'

The IFSC was an Irish offspring of the Big Bang, the mass deregulation and expansion of the finance business, led by the City of London and Wall Street. Within a few years the IFSC had thousands of employees; it was enticing financial outfits from all over the world. The ratings companies were happy with this, as they were happy with the risky new financial instruments being peddled by shysters in sharp suits and red braces. The ratings companies were paid by the people they were 'rating'. They saw nothing wrong with anything, until everything went pear-shaped. To the ratings companies, everything is always AAA, until it's blatantly not, and they adjust their ratings to fall in line with reality.

Ireland, along with Luxembourg and the Channel Islands, was now competing with the Caymans, Bermuda and the Virgin Islands as a handmaiden of the wealthy – and the wealthy expect sweeteners. American companies, for instance, were appreciative of the relaxed attitude to 'transfer pricing'. This involves internal pricing arrangements, as goods are sent from one subsidiary to another, and costs and profits are manipulated – essentially to avoid paying US taxes.

This has long had a distorting effect on the Irish measure of GDP. It also distorts the measurement of exports from the country.

Some of the world's biggest companies began exploiting this tax dodge, with variations that included the 'double Irish' and the 'double Irish with Dutch sandwich'. Official Ireland began to worry. Irish companies and banks were servicing that kind of carry-on and Ireland's growing cowboy reputation might do long-term damage.

Not to worry.

The government came up with the Companies (Audit and Accounting) Act 2003. This required directors of companies over a certain size, and their auditors, to sign some forms each year. No big deal. Just a statement that effective controls were in place to ensure that laws were observed and taxes were paid. It wasn't that regulation was getting any heavier, it was just an effort to show that the government wasn't totally negligent.

Of course, the government has limited sovereignty over the business world. The usual defenders of the free market, of leaving the entrepreneur free to imagine and create, unleashed a barrage of opposition. The government backed off. An ineffective substitute was found, to give the impression that something was being done.

Some saw a Wild West reputation as unfortunate. Others saw a reputation for light-touch regulation as the Dublin financial centre's unique selling point.

There was anecdotal evidence of German financial outfits that didn't dare carry out certain transactions within the regulated German framework. Simple solution: set up an outfit in the IFSC, registered as an Irish entity. When you've got something to do that you can't do in Germany, you hop on a plane to Dublin, to the office of the Irish-registered outfit, carry out the transaction there, then fly home. There was no shortage of professionals ready to oil the mechanism, if you greased their palms.

Michael Gass, head of securities litigation and enforcement at an American law firm, suggested that foreign companies were coming to Ireland 'to set up offices and get away with doing things they would not be able to do elsewhere'.

Jim Stewart, from TCD's School of Business, wrote about the ease with which financial outfits could register in Dublin. Want to move an investment fund to the IFSC? To quote Stewart: 'if the relevant documents are provided to the regulator by 3.00 pm, the fund will be authorised the next day'. This, despite the fact that 'a prospectus for a quoted instrument is a complex legal and financial document' and can run to in excess of two hundred pages.

Of course, regulating the corporate world, making sure that those working in it sign the proper forms and operate within the regulations, is just one aspect of regulation. There's also the enforcement end of things. When things go wrong, there has to be a sheriff who faces down the bad guys.

And Ireland had an efficient sheriff: Paul Appleby, the Director of Corporate Enforcement. His outfit, the Office of the Director of Corporate Enforcement (ODCE), investigated suspected wrongdoing and put things right. The ODCE was set up in 2001. In 2006, it had just thirty-six employees, including six gardaí, and the workload was heavy. Appleby had long known they needed more staff.

It made sense. Financial companies could hire legions of lawyers to trawl the law books for loopholes. Without more ODCE staff, cases would be lost or dropped; more cases simply wouldn't be launched. Appleby wanted twenty more staffers, with particular skills – including four gardaí.

That year alone, the ODCE dealt with 556 cases of questionable loans. These are internal loans taken out by company directors who see their companies as personal piggy banks. The amount involved was €244 million. The ODCE retrieved €160 million and another €48 million of the loans were referred to Revenue for investigation.

At that stage, the ODCE had taken 400 directors to court. They secured 130 convictions, disqualified 1,600 directors and restricted another 680 from company involvement. They had cautioned 900 company directors.

The ODCE's accounts that year, covering 2005, showed that its budget was a measly €4.5 million. This was an office that was supposed to police countless transactions by thousands of financial outfits.

ODCE salaries and allowances totalled €1.8 million. Another €1.1 million went on running the office. Which left €1.6 million to spare. Couldn't the ODCE spend that hiring staff? No. It needed the permission of the government to do that, and it didn't have that permission. So, it had to hand the €1.6 million back to the state.

The ODCE was clearly paying for itself several times over, each year. The small investment needed to increase the staff would more than pay for itself in the money it would save private companies and the state.

Two years after Appleby applied for staff, nothing had happened. Through Freedom of Information requests, RTÉ found out about the delays. Because of the headlines that followed, the authorities conceded that the ODCE should have an increase in staff – four, instead of the requested twenty.

It was the taoiseach himself, Bertie Ahern, who rejected the request, speaking somewhat waspishly in the Dáil. 'He has thirty-six, so it seems extraordinary that he could want another twenty.'

The fact that the ODCE needed the staff to do its job didn't seem to matter; nor that this was an important job, underwriting the credibility of a multibillion-euro business. Ahern seemed to believe that any improvement in staffing should be in small numbers, as a matter of principle.

'One would not receive such an increase in any department,' Ahern said. 'He will have to wait his turn.'

The taoiseach seemed indignant. He pointed out that there had been an increase in the number of labour inspectors.

This was bizarre. The labour inspectors, too, were overworked and under-resourced, but they had nothing to do with the ODCE. It was like turning down a request for urgently needed fire engines on the basis that there had been an increase in the number of ambulances.

Having waited two years for urgently needed staff, the ODCE now found Ahern telling the Dáil that the ODCE could 'wait a few more years if the staff are required'.

By now the political parties that made up the government were true believers in the cult of neoliberalism. Light-touch regulation was as precious to them as the sacraments are to the College of Cardinals. Add to that, a simple deference. It's not often remarked upon, but it is blatant – Official Ireland's humility when dealing with wealth and power. Perhaps it's ingrained from the subservient attitudes of colonial days.

In 2006, as the bubble stretched towards bursting point, we had a regulatory system that wasn't up to the job – because the people who made crucial decisions didn't want it to be up to the job. They just wanted something that would pass for a regulatory system, if you didn't look too closely at it.

Later, the European Central Bank would use the fact of 'light-touch' regulation to legitimize imposing austerity on Irish citizens, and paying bondholders who had made bad bets. Bureaucrats such as Lorenzo Bini Smaghi argued that if the citizens voted for politicians who tolerated inefficient regulation then the citizens had to take responsibility for the consequences. How ordinary citizens would keep track of the technical policies employed in regulating banks was not explained.

However, at EU level, there was no secret about what was going on. At a euro conference in New York, Charlie McCreevy boasted: 'As Finance Minister in Ireland I saw what great entrepreneurial energies a light-touch regulatory system can unleash.' This speech was in April 2005. 'Economic freedom through low taxes, open borders, good corporate governance, and light-touch regulation has been absolutely indispensable to the scale of the success we have seen.' He was speaking as an EU Commissioner, urging other Very Important People to agree that 'the cost of regulation has to be reduced'.

Jean Claude Trichet, head of the European Central Bank, came to Dublin in May 2004. No other individual in Europe had as much information on which to base a judgement on what was happening. There was no way that European banks could gamble €100 billion on the Irish property bubble without their national regulators and the ECB knowing what was going on.

Trichet spoke admiringly of Ireland as 'a model for the millions of new citizens of the European Union'. He applauded the 'astonishing experience of Ireland' and the 'impressive pace of economic activity'. And, of course, the 'sound fiscal position'.

'Ireland,' he noted, had 'developed a transparent regulatory framework.'

Given what was about to happen to the euro, it's worth noting that Trichet was thrilled about the fact that 'we Europeans have been very bold in creating a single currency in the absence of a political federation, a federal government and a federal budget at the euro area level'. He noted that 'some observers' were 'arguing that without a federal budget it would be impossible to weather, with the help of the fiscal channel, asymmetric shocks hitting one particular member economy'.

And that was precisely what was building up under his nose – in Ireland, in Greece, in Spain, in Portugal, in Italy – as he and his highly paid and widely lauded staff presided over neoliberal Europe.

So, we've got deferential politicians, a culture of entrepreneur worship, free-wheeling banks – well, at least the wealth trickled down and ensured the state could provide world-class facilities for its citizens . . .

11

We All Partied

It was 2004 and Ireland had the second highest GDP per person in the European Union. Unemployment was down to around 4 per cent. Our politicians were never done high-fiving one another and patting themselves on the back.

This was right smack in the middle of the period of greatest wealth. Mary Harney had put it well some time earlier: 'The country is awash with money.' At the height of the boom, in this abundantly wealthy country, in one unexceptional week in February 2004, the following came to light in media reports.

An elderly woman, very ill, went to Monaghan Hospital. From there she was sent to Cavan Hospital. And Cavan Hospital sent her back to Monaghan Hospital. She died shortly afterwards. She was seriously ill, she was old – she probably would have died anyway. But that's not the best way to spend your final hours, bouncing like a pinball from one hospital to another, in need of help.

When a public health system is historically underfunded, there is no slack. A slight pressure here leads to a bottleneck somewhere else. Political decisions made on staffing and capacity mean that at the sharp end of the health service everything is a judgement call. When waves of people in trouble overwhelm the system, cracks open up. People tumble through those cracks.

One family mourned a nine-year-old who went into hospital with abdominal pains, was diagnosed with 'tummy bug', was sent home and died. Another family mourned the baby who was tested for meningitis and found negative, was sent home, and died of meningitis.

In the Mater Hospital, in Dublin, a neurological consultant declared the A&E unit to be 'unsafe'. Elsewhere that day, the Irish Nurses Organization spent five hours in a meeting, successfully putting pressure on the authorities to open 96 hospital beds that were closed the previous year. A small victory. Now, there was just another 2,804 beds to find, to make up the 3,000-bed shortage that even the Minister for Health agreed existed.

There was a bizarre moment during all this that explains how our political leaders see things. At the beginning of April 2005, Minister for Health Mary Harney addressed the annual conference of the Irish Medical Association. This was reported in a 2006 book titled *How Ireland Cares*, by Dale Tussing and Maev-Ann Wren. The book quoted Harney telling delegates that:

> [W]e spend 7 per cent more in real terms than the Blair government in Britain. This is 9 per cent per capita more than the Germans and 70 per cent more than the Italians. Only Denmark and Luxembourg are ahead of us.

The book goes on:

> The Department of Health later explained: The Tánaiste did not deliver a scripted speech at the IMO conference in Killarney, as often is her preference. In relation to some

statistics, she was speaking from memory of an article she wrote for the *Irish Times* in October 2003.

Amazingly, Harney was winging it. Depending on her memory of a newspaper article she had written – or someone had written for her – two and a half years earlier.

Tussing and Wren pointed out that 'the Minister was referring to an outdated forecast of health spending in 2003, not 2005'. They continued: 'Ireland's total health spending per capita was at most 82 per cent of the German level, and ranked eight of fourteen EU states.'

The point here is not that Harney made a mistake. It illustrates the way members of that government were removed from reality. They had so often told their fairy tale of achievement, they were so convinced of their own neoliberal mission, that they could in all sincerity spout delusional nonsense.

Complacency at the top and chaos down below.

There was a history of underfunding, often because the state was broke, sometimes because the politicians were passionate about limiting the role of the state. Staff were cut, people retired or moved on and were not replaced. Some who planned to enter the health system had to emigrate and use their training elsewhere. Such cuts had both immediate and long-term effects.

In July 2000, experienced social worker Kieran McGrath commented on a shocking case of a sixteen-year-old who was sleeping rough, having been raped and tortured by her father. 'The origin of the present crisis in child care can, in fact, be traced right back to the cutbacks that were imposed on health boards in the late 1980s, the period of financial rectitude that is now hailed as the foundation of our much vaunted economic miracle.'

The austerity of the past was creating new victims a decade later. Just as the current austerity will cause harm into the future.

The problems in the public health system were often chalked up as examples of incompetence, of the need for reform – and, at the top, there's no doubt that a succession of unfortunates left a trail of damage in its wake. But the political strategy for the health service, widely supported within the Dáil, was one of turning health into a business, not a service. Tax incentives encouraged the consolidation of the private health business, with speculators, lawyers and meat-company executives popping up as hospital owners.

These people didn't suddenly get an urge to play doctor. The problems and under-resourcing in the public service were driving citizens into buying private health care – and that created an opportunity for profit.

Whatever about the unfortunates who mismanaged aspects of the public service, at least they were trying to run a service. The private-sector investors went into the health business to make money. The health service was being reconfigured to suit the investment needs of the speculator class.

Labour Party TD Brendan Howlin, now one of the government's chief enforcers of austerity, was Minister for Health in 1993/4. It wasn't until much later, he told Maev-Ann Wren, who interviewed him for her 2003 book *Unhealthy State*, that he got a perspective on what had been happening. He had never thought through 'in a structured way' the clash between public and private health services.

> I was content to feel that we could provide a first-class public health system, without realising that if we did that, there would be no reason for sustaining a private system . . .
>
> The government wanted a chunk of the population – 30 per cent or thereabouts – to pay for private health insurance but, in order for that to happen, they really

required the public system to be inferior. Why else, if it
was first rate, would people pay for a private system?

Out in Ballymun, the public health centre that cost €48 million
to build lay idle. It would take another €8 million to fit it out, but
there wasn't a spare €8 million in a country that paid its taoiseach
more than prime ministers and presidents across the globe – and
where speculators were making millions from ill health.

The waiting list for serious operations had a couple of thousand
people who had been waiting for over two years.

In Cork, nurses in A&E counted twenty-nine people lying on
trolleys.

In Limerick A&E, thirty-three patients lay on trolleys.

In St James, in Dublin, forty-one patients lay on trolleys.

Down in Wexford, elective surgery was cancelled.

Nurses' representatives described the overcrowding as 'recur-
ring and endemic'.

Around the same period, patients at Dublin's Beaumont could
only dream of the delightful era when you'd have a trolley to lie on in
A&E. One evening there weren't enough beds open in the hospital,
A&E was so crowded they'd run out of trolleys to treat everyone
inside, so patients had to lie on stretchers, in three ambulances
in the car park. Three of the city's ambulances were tied up at
Beaumont, sparing patients from having to lie on the ground.

It could have been any hospital. Having the hospitals working
on a knife edge was government policy. This, they believed, would
produce the 'reforms' the system needed.

Out in Tallaght, a man kicked up a row in A&E. His nineteen-
year-old son had arrived with symptoms of meningitis and was
declared an 'urgent' case. He had been waiting in pain, for five
hours. The row led to the young man being seen. He was diagnosed
with meningitis and he survived.

A seventeen-year-old boy, suffering brain damage, was reckoned to be a danger to himself and to others. The health service had nowhere to treat him. He was sent to prison.

This wasn't an unusually bad week. This was normality in the land of the Celtic Tiger, where swanky department stores had waiting lists for handbags that cost thousands of euro.

Almost a year earlier, in 2003, there were strenuous denials that emergency patients at Tallaght Hospital had been treated in a mortuary room.

It was true, though, that when A&E was under pressure, and the wards were full, and there was nowhere else to put them, patients had to be sent to the room in question. And treated there. And it was true that the room in question was the room where they sometimes put dead people. And it was true that the room in question was known within the hospital as 'The Mortuary'. Apart from that, you could fairly claim that no patients were treated in the mortuary – in the sense that no patients seem to have been treated in that room alongside actual corpses.

Meanwhile, helicopters criss-crossed the sky, ferrying the rich from board meetings to racecourses, from airports to yachts. Gated communities were built so one need not even see, much less engage with, the riff-raff. Cars were imported in sizes appropriate to the vulgar mansions for which the speculators were charging millions. At the top of the pile, some had their own jets; more than a couple of dozen of the richest owned golf courses.

Layers of underlings – lawyers, accountants, consultants of various stripes, PR mouthpieces – were paid appropriate gross premiums for servicing the elite. Their contemporaries in health, architecture and engineering insisted on being equally well rewarded.

University bigwigs saw themselves as educational CEOs, and

were paid accordingly. CEOs and senior executives of private companies added bonuses, share options, dividends and pensions on top of their rock-star wages.

The politicians, who encouraged all this as a sign of national resurgence, weren't shy. They ramped up their own pay and pensions. The civil-service elite and the heads of state companies saw no reason why they shouldn't be the equals of the vastly overpaid private-sector executives.

As for the bankers, their bonuses got bonuses, while the size of their pensions almost matched that of their egos. All this for dim gobshites whose chief talent was the ability to borrow and lend money in a global credit boom.

If you asked for a loan you got a loan. Even if you didn't ask for a loan the banks would offer you one. Ordinary bank depositors got offers in the post, telling them they'd been pre-approved for a loan of ten grand. If you ignored that you got another letter telling you that you'd been pre-approved for a loan of twenty grand.

Some bank customers noticed that their credit limit had gone from a couple of thousand to eight thousand, without even asking.

The media was full of experts telling us that if we didn't borrow now – when interest rates were so low that the banks were practically giving money away – it was because we lacked the spirit necessary to thrive in the land where the Celtic Tiger ran free.

Despite all this, most people remained cautious. But many were tempted to try their hands at imitating the wealthy, buying flats in Eastern Europe and shopping in New York. In what was a noisy, boastful, vulgar scene, the cocaine business thrived.

The media, delighted to have a new set of VIP nonentities, approvingly covered the mundane carousing of large numbers of uncelebrated celebrities, their unremarkable liaisons and their desperate need for attention.

When they turned up at nightclubs, their handbags cost more

than some people's cars. When they went on holiday, their suitcases cost more than most of us spent on a week in the sun.

It seemed as if at the top of every business there was a layer of executives who couldn't do their jobs unless they were sitting on a cushion of money. A big wage wasn't enough, a wage bigger than that of two other people wasn't enough. These people were so lacking in motivation that they required fifteen or twenty times the wage that other people got before they could bother their arses to do their jobs.

Incredibly, these people weren't happy unless they got big bonuses for doing jobs they were already overpaid to do. Those who support the bonus culture are essentially arguing for a complete lack of loyalty to employers. Without bonuses on top of huge wages and extensive perks, you should not feel 'incentivized' enough to do your job properly.

Any worker at shop-floor level who behaved in this way would be sacked – and no union could possibly put up a defence. There was no logic to the big-bucks-and-bonus culture, but logic didn't have anything to do with it. It was the culture of stuffing your face. So many self-important entrepreneurial wannabes were like kids let loose in a chocolate factory.

The neoliberal victory was total – not just economically and politically, but culturally. Dissent had been de-legitimized. The media, feasting on the pickings from property advertising, was saturated with approving descriptions of the new elite. You could moan about the vulgarity of it all, the gross inequality, but that kind of talk was dismissed as the begrudgery of losers.

And, in the brave new world of the Celtic Tiger, losers were people without the wit or the gumption to choose to be a winner.

On the evening of 9 March 2001, as the entrepreneurial classes were practising their *vroom-vroom* noises, a woman we will call Mary arrived at the A&E department of one of our leading hospitals. Again, it could have been any high-pressure hospital.

It's not known how Mary ended up there, as she had not suffered an accident, nor was she an emergency case. She was eighty; she had suffered a turn of some sort. It was late at night and someone sent for an ambulance and there she was.

She was confused. She told the nurses she was sixty-two.

Under pressure, the staff decided she might require psychiatric help, so she was sent to a mental hospital. There, it was decided that, while she was confused, she was not mentally ill. She was sent back to the A&E.

Mary was put on a trolley.

To lie on a trolley for an hour, with a busy staff unable to give you personal care, is a dreadful experience for anyone, let alone an eighty-year-old, baffled, disoriented, frightened person. A&E was busy, noisy, a lot going on.

At 1 a.m. the following day, twenty-four hours after her admission, Mary was still there on the trolley. She lay there through all the hours of the night, the changes of shift, all the events of the day.

She wasn't moved to a bed in a ward because every bed was needed; people who had medical problems had priority. Mary couldn't be sent home, as she hadn't been assessed, no one knew the source of her confusion, and sending her home might not be safe. The hospital hadn't the resources to explore the woman's problem and deal with it – but they weren't going to kick her out to flounder alone. They did what they could.

She was moved, on the trolley, to a space between the cubicles, a kind of wide corridor.

She was still there after another twenty-four hours, forty-eight hours after she had arrived.

Staff didn't ignore her. Since there was no room in any of the hospital wards, they had tried to get her a bed somewhere else. There wasn't one.

She was still there on the trolley twenty-four hours later, seventy-two hours after she had arrived. Three days.

By now she had received visitors, professional carers. She was thirsty. Getting the attention of a nurse, for a glass of water, or a visit to the toilet, wasn't easy. Not when the staff are run off their feet, and the old woman wasn't fully aware of her surroundings.

Her visitors got her 7Up.

Lying on a trolley, between cubicles, with no bedside table, totally dependent on the overworked staff, where do you put your bottle of 7Up?

You have someone put it on the floor. Reaching down every time you need a sip isn't really on, even for a young, physically able, mentally alert person. You have to wait to ask someone to help.

Mary was still on the trolley after another twenty-four hours, ninety-six hours after she had arrived. Four days.

All through the night again, all through the day. Patients were brought through the space between the cubicles, on their way for treatment. Who knows what traumas occurred, how many accident cases, how many deaths, how many old people prayed, how many young people in vomit-flecked clothes sobbed into disposable sheets. Who knows what Mary thought of it all. She didn't even have a wall to turn her face to.

Another twenty-two hours passed, then Mary was found a bed in a ward. She had been on a trolley for three hours short of five days, in a public health system she had helped build, with her decades of work and taxes.

And the condition of the hospitals was no secret.

In 2006, actor Brendan Gleeson went on *The Late Late Show*. This was not a shallow display of celebrity compassion; Gleeson's deeply personal anger was unmistakeable. His mother, father and mother-in-law had been through the hospital mill and he was shaken by it. He likened the A&E to a military field hospital, with overworked staff trying to hold things together. One toilet, people spending days on a trolley and, when they go to the toilet, the trolley is taken for someone else.

'It's disgusting that we're allowing people to die when we have *billions*.'

Gleeson was wrong on that. *We* didn't have the billions. The billions were borrowed by Irish bankers, from European bankers, and doled out to rich people who built what was profitable, encouraged by government tax breaks. We never owned the billions. We never had the use of them. But when the time came we would be handed the burden of paying them back.

Gleeson described his mother-in-law's time in an oncology suite, dying. With the Minister for Health's name on a nearby plaque.

'There were people on chairs, with grieving people, there were people who were trying to fight for life and cling on to hope, beside people who were dead – and this moron's name on a plaque.'

Disgusting conditions, he said. 'Anybody who votes for this crowd to get back next time might as well shoot themselves. I'll be honest with you, I don't think much of the other crowd either.'

To vote these people back, he said, would be like 'somebody comes into the room and started punching your mother and father around the room – and you went up and patted them on the back'.

Gleeson's outburst brought forth waves of support. By now, there was widespread awareness of what the running down of the public health service meant for the citizens.

The following year, there was a general election. The choice was between the people who were in charge of an allegedly booming economy and the people who said they'd do it better.

And, for a third time, the voters elected the Ahern/Harney

free-market extremists. 'Went up,' as Brendan Gleeson put it, 'and patted them on the back.'

Like Gleeson, the voters didn't 'think much of the other crowd either'. Unlike Gleeson, not enough believed that radical change was needed, or possible.

12

Watching the Money Flow

HERE'S THE THING THAT explains a lot: the *flow* of the money. Not just the fact that there was a lot of money about, but where it came from and where it went, and why. How it flowed into and out of the country, and what it did while it was here.

The frenzy that occurred wasn't just about Fianna Fáil pumping the bubble, nor about the recklessness and greed of the likes of Sean FitzPatrick. They're part of the story, and not the most important part. The recklessness was important, and it was extraordinary, but that's not what this is about. The fortunes won and lost are of interest to all of us, the gamblers and their misadventures are at times fascinating – but that's mere soap opera.

The story of what happened, and the story of the desperate fix we're in today – and where we might go from here – is about the *flow of money.*

By 2004, we'd been through a boom and a minor slump. When things slowed down after 9/11, the Fianna Fáil/PD government tightened spending. They believed that was the right thing to do, because they believed their own legends. The lesson they'd taken from the 1980s was that when times get tough, you cut services.

Expansionary fiscal contraction.

Those who made fortunes in the good times were protected. Citizens depending on services and benefits saw them cut when they needed them most – after paying for them through the decades in which they worked.

As the economy revved up again, everyone was looking for a piece of the good times. The share of the national cake going to labour had gone down during the 1990s boom; the share going to capital had risen. Now there was a demand for more fairness, and wages were pushed up.

The population was increasing, the workforce expanding, more women were working, Irish emigrants came home, foreign immigrants came here to work. There was increased demand for housing.

In 2000, as a result of the boom, 50,000 houses had been completed. At the height of the bubble in 2006, the number was 93,000. By 2007, over 13 per cent of all employment was in construction.

Not only were there far more houses being built, but they were also far more expensive, as prices lost any connection to reality. From 1996 to 2007, house prices quadrupled.

And quality tumbled.

From very early on, it wasn't hard to spot the lousy workmanship in the apartments being flung up in record time. Eventually, the desperate stories emerged as people found they'd taken out mortgages on homes with crappy finishes that quickly deteriorated. Worse still, some were fire hazards, others had been built using pyrite, which led to widening cracks, floors that moved, doors that stuck.

The banks, up to 2003, had kept some relationship between the money they were taking on deposit and the money they were lending. That sanity was about to unravel.

Where did the money come from, to fund the Irish bubble?

Money never sleeps; it doesn't just sit in an account. It has to flow to somewhere, to work for its owners, and to bring back a flow of profit. Europe, at that stage, had huge differences in accumulated wealth. In Germany, for instance, wages had been held down for a long time, the banks and finance houses had amassed huge investment funds on behalf of their wealthy clients.

Their fund managers prowled the world, looking for opportunities. They saw the billions being made on the Irish property game, and they wanted in on the act.

Interest rates were set by the European Central Bank (ECB), which cared most about the health of the bigger economies. And the bigger economies favoured a low interest rate. The long-term effect of low interest rates on smaller economies such as Ireland was deemed to be of secondary importance – if anyone at the ECB thought of it at all.

Low interest rates meant cheap loans. The people who claim to know about these things were all over the media, telling us it was practically criminal not to borrow at such low rates. The bankers, their paid mouthpieces and their unpaid cheerleaders, the money experts, the consultants and the construction-industry shills, the councillors re-zoning like mad, the national politicians organizing tax breaks – all pounding home the message that you'd better get on to the property ladder before it was too late.

The notion of the property ladder, the need to get on to it, the need to climb it, saturated the culture. The newspapers played it up, and made a lot of money from property advertising. Television made a game show of it.

Those who had bought land cheap and hoarded it now made a killing. The speculators thrived, the builders, the estate agents, the banks.

Spending only what you earned or saved was the mark of a loser.

People with initiative took advantage of the cheap money to leverage their equity.

We didn't have houses any more, we had *equity*.

We didn't borrow, we *leveraged*.

Like 'punching above our weight', 'leverage' was part of the jargon that made some people feel like something magical was happening. You owed it to yourself to grasp your destiny as a 'risk taker'. Borrowing, taking on a debt, used to be a negative thing. Now, you were *leveraging*, and that was a positive, a sign of entrepreneurial initiative.

As house prices rose, your house became worth more than you paid for it. In theory, you could sell it and make a bundle. In theory, we were all suddenly rich, without having to lift a finger. Just sit there in your house and get rich. In practice, if you sold your house you'd have to pay as much or more for somewhere else to live. The wealth was imaginary.

So, people learned some more jargon of the new age of financial magic: you should, they were told, 'release the equity' in your house. The bankers made it seem like your attic was full of fluttering banknotes, yearning for you to punch a hole through the roof, so they could fly away and procreate. In fact, all it meant was you were borrowing more, to spend on immediate needs, or to gamble on another property.

In theory, had the Irish state been able to set its own interest rates, the worst of the collapse might have been averted. Interest rates would have been pushed up, putting the brakes on the economy, slowing the borrowing, easing the bubble that followed.

An honest appraisal, however, would have to conclude that even if McCreevy and Cowen and Harney and Ahern and their Central Bankers had the power to do that, they'd still have let the economy rip.

The world of cheap loans and building booms was a politician's wet dream. These guys believed – or wanted to believe – they'd found the promised land, where cheap money unleashed the entrepreneurial talents of a people who had finally taken their place among the nations of the Earth.

Cool the economy? That would be like asking Winnie the Pooh to take it easy on the honey.

An utter flood of money came into the country, from foreign investors seeking to profit from the Irish boom. In 2003, the Irish banks owed €15 billion in bonds issued to international investors, the bankers in Germany, the UK, France and elsewhere. Just four years later, they had borrowed €100 billion in such bonds.

Remember that economist back in Chapter 7 who told the *Irish Times*, 'The Tiger's back, *vroom-vroom*'? That was in July 2004 – just as that astonishing wave of money hit the country.

Let's watch the money flow.

It flowed from the German, and other, banks, into the Irish banks. By the end of 2008, an average of €20 billion per quarter was flowing from German banks alone to what would become the stressed economies of Greece, Italy, Portugal, Spain and Ireland. One analysis showed that, 'Net capital flows from Germany to Ireland increased sharply between 2006 and late 2008.' Tens of billions flowed into this country.

From there, the money went in three directions.

Direction one. It went to the builders and speculators, to throw up housing estates anywhere they could get land. Doesn't matter if there are services available, doesn't matter if you're building on a flood plain, doesn't matter if it's miles from anywhere. Build it and they will come.

The same builders and speculators got money from the banks for anything they imagined they could flog on to the commercial sector – a hotel, a car park, an office block, an apartment building with retail shops on the ground floor.

Direction two. The people buying the houses (whether as a home or to let) got money from the banks to buy mortgages. They tied themselves into, perhaps, a 100 per cent mortgage, some over a period of thirty years. Many of those who already owned homes believed the bankers when they claimed that the smart thing to do was to 'release the equity' in their homes, by topping up their mortgage.

By 2005, a third of all loans were mortgage top-ups. This came to €5 billion annually.

Direction three. The firms buying the commercial buildings got money from the banks to buy mortgages.

As the money flowed, some of it was siphoned off by the estate agents and the land hoarders, the professional classes and the media that sold property adverts.

Pause.

Now, the money begins flowing back.

The monthly interest payments on all these mortgages rolled into the Irish banks from the individuals and companies. Bank profits grew, top bankers paid themselves obscene amounts of money.

The rest of the mortgage cash flowed back to the European banks that bought the bonds issued by the Irish banks.

The money flowed into the country and out again, creating huge profits for the bankers – here and abroad – and for the builders and speculators, the professional classes.

The immediate needs of such people, their greed fuelled by government tax breaks, distorted and undermined the real economy. Had a fraction of that money been invested in building a working public health system, a well-resourced, forward-looking education system, useful and sustainable business – rather than gambling on a bubble – the country would look very different.

But the country isn't designed for that, it's designed to meet the immediate needs of a thin layer of people, and their cheerleaders and hangers-on.

And as the global credit freeze arrived, and the waves of money retreated, the gambling splurge left behind countless badly built houses, ghost estates, hotels and office buildings no one needed – and from which a lot of people made a lot of money.

And, as the waves of money retreated, they also left behind an enormous, ever-expanding shit-pile of debt.

In theory, this shit-pile of debt was underwritten by enormous amounts of very valuable Irish property. It was soon clear, however, that this property was deliriously overvalued – by the people who made fortunes from assuring everyone those valuations were real.

The bankers and speculators, the builders and bondholders were in big trouble. They, the people who had incurred the gambling debts, didn't have, and would never have, enough money to pay them off.

No problem.

Someone else would have to do it.

13

What We Have We Hold

NEVER IN THE HISTORY of the state was there such a period of total, overwhelming panic as that which afflicted the Irish establishment in 2008. The ship of state was steaming towards the rocks, they were pressing all the usual buttons – and nothing worked.

Now, when smart thinking was required, the politicians, top civil servants and bankers were out of their depth. They had demanded and received obese salaries, perks and pensions to match their view of their own value. And when push came to shove they were as useful as chocolate teapots.

They hired platoons of consultants from the big international banks. They paid them millions to advise the government what to do. However, the global banking system was already freezing up. The advisers couldn't be certain that their own firms would make it to the end of the year.

The advisers charged top rates. They made big bucks from the crisis, but the advice they gave was indecisive, and the politicians – well, they mentally flipped a coin and put the entire future of the country on backing the bankers.

The answer you get in any crisis depends on the question you ask. A question the politicians might have asked was: 'How do we best protect the citizens?' The answer would have been complex. It would have required vision and courage. It would have required radical thinking and a break with the values of the old politics.

The question they asked was: 'How do we save the banks?'

This question was entirely in keeping with the politics of the Celtic Bubble. The politicians saw their role as facilitating the interests of the entrepreneurial geniuses – the nexus of bankers, captains of commerce, builders and developers.

These were the people the politicians looked up to, played golf with, received political donations from. These were bankers who took home pay packets worth millions. To the politicians, there was really only one thing to do.

'Here's what we need,' said the bankers.

'Fair enough,' said the politicians.

And they laid more than €400 billion on the line.

Of course, they assured us, we'll never be called on to back up that guarantee.

And Official Ireland cheered. The politicians had saved the day. For quite a while, those who had been cheerleaders for the bubble remained cheerleaders for the bank guarantee.

Eventually, the penny dropped. The responsibility for the shit-pile of debt had been calmly passed from the gamblers to the citizens. The tens of billions needed to save the banks would be sucked out of the public purse.

Minister for Finance Brian Lenihan said: 'We're not rushing into the banks like some governments in other countries without knowing exactly what the situation is in those banks.' This – like much else we were to hear from Official Ireland – was the exact opposite of the truth.

The politicians knew next to nothing about the true state of the banks. Some of the bankers knew next to nothing about the true state of the banks.

Three years later, the electorate would grievously punish Fianna Fáil for this disaster, but the blame spread far wider than those bunglers. Each step along the road to ruin was known at various levels of the Irish and European establishments, and they gloried in it.

The statistics and fact of the credit bubble were available to the Irish Regulator's office, the Central Bank, the Bundesbank, the Banque de France, the Bank of England.

And the German regulators, and the regulators in France and the UK, and so on.

There was nothing going on here in the years to 2008, or in Germany or in France, that was concealed from the leaders of the European Central Bank.

They knew the German, French and other banks were lending extraordinary amounts of money into a property bubble – and they knew they were profiting from it. They must have known of the imbalances caused by the application of a single interest rate across a range of economies with different long- and short-term interests.

What had been happening was known to all their highly paid economists, consultants and analysts.

It was known to the big firms of lawyers and accountants who made spectacular fees from servicing what was happening.

It was known to the auditors and the ratings agencies.

It was known to the specialist media commentators.

All of it was known, understood and cheered.

People who couldn't spell the word 'neoliberal', let alone argue its case, had for years pounded the rest of us with crude triumphalism. The markets had spoken; the entrepreneurs were the winners – because they were the 'wealth creators', the ones who 'created' and 'innovated' (activities that, it turned out, largely involved borrowing more than they could pay back).

The media, which had obediently cheered all this, now denounced any who dared 'talk down the economy'.

Just before the bank guarantee, people rang Joe Duffy's *Liveline* with anecdotal evidence of money being taken out of the banks. The politicians were daily assuring us that the banks were 'well capitalized' and totally safe. All we had to fear was fear itself. The people on the line to Duffy knew different.

In government circles, Simon Carswell later reported, there was anger that 'taxi driver and hairdresser' types were being listened to as though they knew something about the economy. Brian Lenihan rang RTÉ to complain.

As it turned out, taxi drivers and hairdressers had a better idea of what was going on than did the Minister for Finance. Had that controversy over *Liveline* been built on, to discuss the dilemma the politicians were in, if it had been used to bring the citizens into the debate, who knows where that debate might have gone. But such thoughts were repellent to Official Ireland. This was a matter for the bankers and politicians to decide, with consultation with appropriate people at select dinner parties. All others must be shut up. The media largely shrugged in agreement at the snuffing out of the *Liveline* discussion.

Lenihan would later denounce newspaper columnists who expressed opinions on the economy. Such discussion should be limited to the 'very many accomplished specialist columnists in the area of business and economics'. In short, to those who had been cheerleaders for the credit bubble and the bank guarantee.

This was to be a crucial element in the disaster that followed. Despite all, the establishment still saw themselves as capable, diligent, and their confidence in their free-market extremism never wavered.

Of course, there'd been some 'mistakes', a banker or two had perhaps stepped over this line or that. A few got carried away with themselves, perhaps one or two 'accomplished specialist columnists' somewhat misread what was happening.

But, fundamentally, the right people had done okay in the circumstances. And it should be left to the right people to discuss this, to make decisions. The country needed their talents and their patriotism. And the rest of us should do as we are told.

Meanwhile, the wealthy siphoned their money out of the country. Some property speculators moved assets into their wife's name; others began figuring how to move assets out of the reach of creditors. Many began making enquiries about how they might be deemed UK residents so they could avail themselves of the lenient UK bankruptcy laws. The politicians, the bankers, the speculators, the top civil servants, the 'over-leveraged' entrepreneurs and the media insiders all saw the collapse as a bad break from which they and their fortunes would recover.

The road ahead would be tough; the tactics would have to vary. The establishment would have to make some small sacrifices, and the occasional important person who had behaved too blatantly and had become a liability would have to be sacrificed.

But one aim was sacrosanct above all else.

What we have we hold.

However events unfolded, however this ended, the fundamental, structural inequalities must be preserved. The principles of the old politics must be protected.

This was understood at national level, and at European level.

There was no need for a summit meeting or a conference to discuss and agree on this policy. There was no need to announce it. That policy's existence was implicit in everything Official Ireland did as the crisis developed.

Part Two

The Slow Death of
the Old Politics

14

Struggling to be Born

THE ELECTION CENTRES HAD closed an hour earlier, no votes had yet been counted, but everyone knew that Fianna Fáil had got an historic thumping. The polls said it, and reaction to the canvass said it. The party's canvassers had found windows and doors adorned with abusive warnings about the treatment they could expect if they dared ring the bell. That Friday evening, RTÉ's *Eleventh Hour* TV programme featured a number of guests discussing the implications of the February 2011 general election. How would the defeat affect FF? Could they make a comeback? Would Fine Gael get an overall majority, and if they didn't, would Labour join a coalition?

One *Eleventh Hour* guest, Theo Dorgan, stood back from the immediate concerns of the election result and tried to put events in perspective.

'I think we're going through a great change,' he said. 'The Irish people have dealt the first decisive blow to the old politics. The biggest political party and the biggest political organization on the island has been dealt a death blow. And next time out the exact same thing will happen to Fine Gael . . . Nothing in this election has persuaded me that Fianna Fáil, Fine Gael or a great chunk of Labour understands just exactly, truly a) how desperate the situation is, b) how powerless the old politics is to deal with it.'

And the situation was indeed desperate. We were left with around 300,000 vacant units around the country, built as part of the lending war between bankers, the mad decisions of local councils, the greed of speculators and builders and the tax-incentive policies of the government. Almost 3,000 unfinished estates. Almost 24,000 commercial units were vacant, more than twice the normal amount.

Thousands of people who had sought nothing more than a roof over their heads had taken out mortgages to meet the sky-high asking prices – which the experts assured them were good value. They now found themselves in negative equity, trapped in homes worth less than the mortgage they faced paying off over the next couple of decades. Some families, unable to sell the house, would see one or more emigrate in search of work, to keep up the mortgage payments. The roof remained over the family's head, at the cost of the break-up of the family.

Others, who had speculated, bought or built houses, flats, offices, car parks, hospitals, with a view to making a killing, faced a big financial loss. Some of the biggest players were now hunkering down with their legal teams, to see who best they might sue.

Steadily, billion by billion, the politicians continued to shift private losses on to the public balance sheet, racking up insane levels of debt.

Worst of all, the collapse of the property bubble quickly led to astonishing levels of unemployment. From 4 per cent, the jobless figures soared above 14 per cent. Among young men, the unemployment rate grew to around 25 per cent. In the twelve months to April 2009, the number of people who emigrated was 18,400. Over the following two years, the total was 67,900.

Dorgan was assessing the politics of the crisis over a long period. 'I think Fianna Fáil is a dead piece of roadkill at the moment . . . There's going to be, I think, a decimation of Fine Gael the next time out.'

On TV, economists were sometimes asked if this recession was as bad as the one in the 1980s. They invariably stroked their chins and concluded, No, it wouldn't be that bad. Just a bit more of the old belt-tightening and we'd turn the corner. As the wasted years of austerity went on, there was always some highly regarded idiot cheerfully announcing that we would soon 'turn the corner' or 'get back on track'.

These were the same people who had complacently observed the property bubble, then confidently predicted a soft landing. For some reason, the media kept on looking to these wretched losers to explain what was happening to the economy. They could reel off facts and figures and explain, in exquisite technical language, how economics worked, and should work and would work – and they were always wrong.

'People are going through a strange, slow-motion crash of the state,' Dorgan suggested. 'They've dealt with one of the great monoliths. They're now scrupulously giving the other monolith in the old politics its shot. And when that proves itself – as it absolutely will, I'm completely certain of this – a busted flush, then the new politics will happen. So it seems to me this is an interim moment in a long, unfolding process of change.'

Very slow change, as it turned out.

When the government knew the banks were in trouble, from early 2008, they responded as they were bound to. All their political, economic, cultural and personal experience and beliefs told them to save the banks, at any cost.

Brian Cowen: 'You write whatever cheques you have to write in the interests of maintaining the financial stability of the state.' Even though the banks, and the cheques Cowen was writing for them, would undermine the stability of the state, for politicians such as Cowen, Lenihan and the Kennys and Gilmores who followed them, doing otherwise was not an option.

The crisis was so big, the threat to the citizens so grave, that truly radical choices needed to be made. Any politician worthy of a vote knew that urgent questions were being forced on to the agenda. What were banks for? Did we need massive banks recklessly borrowing to recklessly invest in one bubble after another? What was the proper function of banks, what did we, the citizens – not the bankers, not the speculators, not the gamblers – need from banks?

There is no evidence that any such questions were even considered, at any time, as the politicians broke up the family furniture, to toss it on the fire that might keep the dying banks warm.

The truth is simple and obvious: decades of stagnant politics have left us with bog-standard right-wing politicians who see the world in very limited terms. Give them standard decisions to make, within the narrow range they're used to, and they're fine. In a crisis, with the best will in the world, they're incapable of doing anything other than pushing the usual buttons. And when nothing happens, they push them again and again and again – the definition of mediocrity being that you do the same thing over and over, expecting different results.

Brian Cowen notoriously thumped the table. 'We're not fucking nationalizing Anglo!'

Nationalizing a collapsing bank is a standard technique within capitalism. It's what the Swedes did, in the early 1990s crisis. For Cowen and his contemporaries, even that small, tactical step was too radical. The old politics said no, no, no.

That night of the election, Theo Dorgan remained hopeful. 'A new way of thinking is struggling to be born. And it's not ready yet to be cut off at the neck and co-opted by the spinmeisters and by the image makers.'

At the same time, the old politics was assembling its forces.

'You now have an alignment between senior managers in the public service,' Dorgan said, 'senior managers in the private sector, senior politicians, senior civil servants – and senior media figures.'

It was worse than that. Official Ireland had for years tolerated a system riddled with corruption. Those who were not corrupt turned blind eyes to corruption in others, rather than let the institutions be discredited. Just like the bishops did when faced with child abuse.

From land purchases, through planning, building, selling and taxing – at all stages there were chancers looking for a backhander; from housing estates built where no one wanted to live to shopping centres diverted from where they were badly needed; a corrupt payment here, a case file closed over there, a loophole found. Bankers aiding fraud, Revenue making deals with fraudsters, the collaboration of lawyers and accountants. From Charlie Haughey's office to councillors huddled in Conway's Pub, from similar huddles in the bar of the Shelbourne Hotel to the Cayman Islands – wherever Official Ireland prospered, envelopes were passed, ears were whispered into, corruption flourished.

The old politics had eventually crashed the country. But there was no new politics credible enough to take on the task of rebuilding. So the old politics hung on: the same people, the same policies, the same cheerleaders. And the austerity regime they enforced made the economy weaker.

The new ways of thinking, beyond the limits of the corrupt old politics, were still struggling to be born. Citizens were still shocked by the crash, still afraid, still hoping the new Fine Gael/Labour government would have something new to offer.

The old politics, however, had already hit the ground running.

The first thing they did was blame us.

'We decided as a people, collectively, to have this property boom,' said Brian Lenihan. 'That was a collective decision we took as a people.' According to Lenihan, 'We all partied.'

Martin Mansergh: 'I think there's maybe been some imprudence, with the benefit of hindsight, on the part of us all.'

Enda Kenny: 'People simply went mad, borrowing.'

Dermot Gleeson, chairman of Allied Irish Banks (AIB): 'As a nation we abetted a number of falsehoods . . . The feel-good factor was allowed to outweigh rationality.'

Arm in arm, it seems, factory and office workers decided with millionaire developers to build ghost estates in the middle of bogs. The unemployed joined Mr Lenihan in agreeing to guarantee all the lousy gambles the bankers made. Small business people joined with bankers such as Mr Gleeson to abet falsehoods and outweigh reality, did they?

The second thing the old politics did was insist that since we all went mad and partied, it was we who should pick up the bill – and the austerity regime began.

15

The Theology of Austerity

THE FIRST EFFECTIVE SHOT in the austerity wars was fired – incredibly – by none other than Sean FitzPatrick, Chairman of Anglo Irish Bank.

Here's FitzPatrick, speaking at a function in September 2005, and reported in the *Irish Times*. It was at a time when his God-awful bank was running up unsustainable levels of borrowing from abroad and lending to developers:

> It was as if, overnight, we discovered just how good we were. We were bright, well educated, flexible, good-natured, creative and even hardworking. The Paddy stopped drinking G&Ts before the three-course, three-hour lunch and found Ballygowan, the bowl of soup and the hang sandwich.
>
> We had ideas, and we had balls . . . And all the time as we worked the scene and maximized the moment, the world watched in astonishment.

It was typical Celtic Tiger-speak. The mock-laddish language ('hang sandwich'), the blatant boasting, the detachment from reality. Then there were the swipes at the media, the cheering for tax breaks and 'incentives' – and the pretence that business had its back against the wall, as grey bureaucrats sought to inflict endless regulation on to free spirits. He warned: 'Moves towards greater control and regulation could squeeze the life out of an economy that has thrived on intuition, imagination and a spirit of adventure.'

The politicians listened; the regulation remained a joke. Meanwhile, the charming Mr FitzPatrick had borrowed up to €122 million from the bank he had the responsibility to run. He wanted those loans to invest in property deals, and – happily – there was a bonus. The politicians had arranged things so that property investors got big tax breaks, which meant FitzPatrick paid less tax on his obscenely large salary.

The conclusion must surely be that FitzPatrick wanted to keep his loans secret. Around September of each year, as the auditors moved in to check Anglo's books, he moved his loans out of the bank. His buddy, Michael 'Mickey Fingers' Fingleton of Irish Nationwide Building Society, kindly 'warehoused' the loans, to keep them secret. And when the auditors were gone, the bankers moved the loans back to Anglo.

On Friday, 3 October 2008, just days after the government gave the bankers the notorious blanket guarantee, FitzPatrick spoke at a seminar in Greystones organized by a local heritage group. The organizers had lots of business connections, so the list of speakers was sprinkled with the movers and shakers of Celtic Tiger Ireland. One of them, developer Sean Mulryan, pulled out at the last moment. Those present included Tom Parlon, former PD minister, now mouthpiece for the construction business, Tom Coffey of the Dublin Business Association and Sean Dunne, speculator extraordinaire.

And what words of wisdom did Mr FitzPatrick have to offer a

nation suddenly afraid, the economic ground crumbling beneath its feet?

He'd like corporation tax cut to 10 per cent, please.

And the government should tackle the 'sacred cow' of child benefits.

And he wasn't happy that all those aged over seventy were entitled to a medical card.

The country, he said, needed clear and courageous leadership.

His Anglo buddy, David Drumm, was just as confident that the populace was up for a blast of austerity. He told the *Financial Times* that the Irish understood 'the need for belt-tightening. We're realists. We knew it couldn't last for ever.'

Mr Drumm was on €3.2 million at the time. This guy could have taken a 95 per cent wage cut and still ended up on a very nice €160,000 a year.

Now, this kind of thing could be seen as the delusional ramblings of bigshots who didn't yet realize the contempt in which they and their views were held. But that wouldn't be true. Taoiseach Brian Cowen was already stoking up the austerity train, and Brian Lenihan brought forward the scheduled budget. And he announced that among the benefits to be cut were child benefits and the over-seventies medical card.

Most of us might see Mr FitzPatrick as a questionable individual who had run his own business into the ground, but to the government he remained a voice worth listening to.

Although the policies of neoliberalism had wreaked havoc in the USA, in Ireland and across Europe, those espousing those policies hadn't gone away. And their core beliefs remained as strong as ever. They still believed in all the stuff about privatization and de-regulation, competitiveness and competition, and giving tax breaks to special people and then hoping the special people would let some wealth trickle down to the rest of us. The politicians among them believed nothing mattered more than cutting deficits – right down to 3 per cent, as the EU wanted.

Most of all, in the teeth of the crisis, they believed in bankers and entrepreneurs. They believed in shifting the burden of the crash on to those on average wages, to free the bankers and entrepreneurs to rebuild the economy.

After all, didn't it work in the 1980s and early 1990s?

Well, not really. There were other things happening back then: billions coming in from EU development funds, the devaluation of the Irish pound, for instance.

The belief in bankers and entrepreneurs, despite all that happened, was semi-religious. It was an article of neoliberal faith; like all faiths, it didn't need evidence to survive. Brian Lenihan, without blushing, could earnestly and sincerely say that his aim was to 'restore the banks to their former greatness'. At that stage, even with the wreckage of the economy all around us, Mr Lenihan still thought of the banks as great institutions – not greed machines with a pick-and-choose attitude to the law.

What we needed was a radical reassessment of where we were. And where we should go. A new way of thinking that threw off the theology of neoliberalism. But vision and courage and new thinking were in short supply among the dominant politicians and their advisers. The old politics – crashed, redundant and incapable – could offer nothing but remedies to restore what it saw as its own 'former greatness'.

The simplistic notion of 'expansionary fiscal contraction', therefore, sprang easily to the lips of Official Ireland. No need for radical change, just the usual cuts inflicted on the low- and medium-paid, the old and the school kids: tighten everyone's belts a little, tighten some people's belts a lot.

And so began, in the wake of Sean FitzPatrick's demand for cuts in social welfare, the era of austerity.

As befits a quasi-religious campaign, the economics of the austerity binge were left pretty vague. These are the things we must do, because these are the things our religious tracts require us to do.

There is some theory behind it.

For instance, take unemployment. When mass unemployment is discussed, Official Ireland usually puts on a sad face and wishes aloud that something could be done about it. It's discussed as though it were a natural disaster – flooding that can't be helped.

In truth, unemployment isn't an accidental by-product of the crisis. According to the theories these people believe in, unemployment is not so much a problem as part of the solution to a bigger problem.

Here's the theory. An austerity policy of charges and taxes and cuts in jobs and services will drive down aggregate demand – the total demand for goods and services. Drive that down, you drive unemployment up, and keep it up.

This should drive down wages.

And prices.

This will, in the jargon of right-wing economists, 'allow the recession to do its work'. In the eyes of such people, a recession isn't an unfortunate collapse, it's a tool.

The recession will wipe out unproductive elements, creating cheaper and more flexible labour. This will allow profit margins to expand, the wealthy will end their investment strike and the recovery will begin.

Meanwhile, we mortgage the future to keep a couple of banks alive – and kiss ass at EU level, in the hope they'll eventually give us a deal on debt – so we can stay this side of bankruptcy.

That's the theory. Just as these people have a semi-religious belief in the infallible power of the market, and the notion of 'expansionary contraction', so do they believe passionately in what they call 'creative destruction'.

So, they got destructive, but it turned out not to be that creative. Year after year of austerity and we're all still in a hole. Nothing changes except it gets deeper.

Not to worry, there's always a pet economist ready to see recovery over the next hill.

And there was a bonus to this austerity thing. Once you could categorize something as a waste of money that we could ill afford in these perilous times – well, it was easy to get rid of. And there were all sorts of things Official Ireland had long wanted to do. Cut back on all that oul' nonsense about combating poverty. And we don't need watchdogs for this and that, the kind of outfits that could embarrass a government. Sell off state properties, marginalize the unions, cut wages and trash working conditions – all part of a neo-liberal wish list from long before the crash.

Within the private sector, some companies did the smart thing. As times remained bad, they tried to hold on to experienced workers. It was foolish to use the recession opportunistically to cut staff and costs: it was a short-term gain for a long-term loss.

The worst of the self-regarding entrepreneurs, however, had a free hand to exploit the high unemployment – all in the name of 'increasing competitiveness'. Not jobs – work. Contract work, part-time work, casual work and work on commission, all designed to extract the most work for the least payment, with the fewest labour rights. You can diligently seek work, then you're supposed to feel grateful when some ruthless gobshite offers you a 'job' at a fiver a day, plus commission.

And the political representatives of the profiteers who cash in on high unemployment bemoan the lack of entrepreneurial spirit in young people who reject such economic abuse.

In presenting an austerity programme as a solution to the crisis, the worst of the worst got to do all sorts of things they'd wanted to do for years, in good times and bad.

And when austerity plainly failed – when the economy remained flat, when unemployment remained obscenely high – the politicians and their pet economists could see that it wasn't working in practice, but, by God, they knew it worked in theory.

So they demanded more austerity.

Because this is not politics, this is not economics – this is a form of religion. Like a Stalinist factory manager insisting that the targets set by the politburo in Moscow must be met, despite famine and lack of raw materials, more hardship is piled on those below. To our Austerity Hawks, reality is what the theory says it is.

There was an example of the semi-religious nature of the old politics in October 2009, at a conference of economists held in Kenmare.

Irish economists are terribly polite. It's a small world, and even when they disagree strongly they tend to do so while fulsomely expressing the greatest respect for one another. There is very little public criticism of even the most outrageous foul-ups.

So when this Kenmare get-together exploded, very little of what happened emerged, and we're dependent on a couple of media reports leaked by some of those attending, in coded, mostly innocuous language. Mostly the economists present were those who had gone along with the bubble, some of them working for the banks. And then there was Morgan Kelly of UCD.

When Kelly emerged from his academic cubby-hole a couple of years before the collapse and said things were looking dire, he was more or less told to bugger off. The taoiseach of the day, a man called Ahern, suggested people like Kelly should commit suicide. When Kelly said – the night after it was given – that the bank guarantee was a mistake, he was publicly laughed at. Now, at this conference, when he bad-mouthed the National Asset Management Agency (NAMA), the government's proposed 'bad bank' solution to the zombie bank crisis – well, that was too much even for some of the terribly, terribly polite Irish economists.

One might suppose that even those who disagreed with Kelly would want to hear him. He wasn't always right about everything, but he was no spoofer. After all, Irish economists are still willing to listen politely to their colleagues who were always wrong about everything.

But, at Kenmare, one economist rose to his feet and condemned the conference organizers for giving Morgan Kelly a platform. Who was this academic to question the orthodoxies of the day regarding property and banking?

Now, Kelly isn't noticeably radical. In most societies he'd be seen as a mainstream academic, teaching the next generation, adding to the sum of human knowledge. Among his conscientiously researched works are 'Market Contagion: Evidence from the Panics of 1854 and 1857', and 'The Poor Law of Old England: Resource Constraints and Demographic Regimes'. He is about learning and understanding and teaching.

Where Kelly differed from most of the economists and politicians of the day was that he looked closely at the evidence and said aloud in plain language what conclusions he drew from this. He did so without filtering everything through an intellectual sieve that discarded material that might offend Official Ireland.

In replying to the chap who questioned his right to address the conference, anecdotal evidence suggests Kelly said something like this: 'Who the fuck am I to express a point of view on property and banking?' He was, he pointed out, the guy who predicted the property collapse. He was the guy who said the banks were insolvent.

Now, what matters is not that Kelly was right and others were wrong. What is revealing is that another economist should question Kelly's presence at the conference. You might imagine that a confident economist would welcome a chance to refute Kelly's views. And this chap was himself an economist held in high regard by bankers, government ministers and the media. He was well able to argue the opposing case.

What was revealing was that this mild, rare expression of a dissenting view was regarded as being so unusual, so worrying – so intolerable. Similarly, when a number of economists and academics raised serious doubts about the government strategy that created NAMA – the bad bank that was going to make everything good – they were treated as though they had farted in church.

Official Ireland was used to talking to itself, to hearing its cheer-leaders applaud, never a strong opposing view. And even after the utter collapse of the neoliberal project the establishment found it hard to tolerate any thinking outside its own narrow limits.

In the media, too, any views that stepped outside the enclosed world of cuts and deficits were declared 'for the birds'. No argu-ment, no thinking, just ideology. This is not within our traditional credo, so it need not be considered.

Such responses to dissidence are not the stuff of economics. They are not the stuff of politics. They are the stuff of religion.

Much of Official Ireland had prided itself on tearing free from the suffocating clutches of institutional Catholicism, in which the word of the bishops was law. But they had dropped one orthodoxy, one ideological comfort blanket, and picked up another. The credo that had brought about the crash was as suffocating, as persistent, as self-protective and as authoritarian as the old theology ever was.

The economic lesson after the Great Depression of the 1930s, taken by the great bulk of economists, was that you can't cut your way out of a recession. When private capital goes on strike, the economy withers; only the state can fill the gap temporarily. If you cut state spending, you affect consumer spending, depress demand, unemployment goes up – and the economy spirals down – and you risk turning a recession into a prolonged depression.

With the defeat of the Keynesian point of view, such views were heresy. A whole generation of economists came to maturity knowing that to challenge the tenets of neoliberalism was as unthinkable as it might have been for a seminarian under Archbishop John Charles McQuaid to question the doctrine of transubstantiation.

The new theology said that there was too much fat in the economy, primarily in the public sector (whatever the statistics might say). The hope was that if you cut severely, taking away services, slashing staffing to the bone, the deficit will come down and there'll still be enough demand to lift the economy.

Cut services, cut benefits – shift the burden to the low- and medium-paid.

They did as their neoliberal religious tenets demanded. And the economy slumped, the predicted growth didn't come, unemployment stayed stubbornly high.

And, as usual with true believers, the failure of the austerity policy was evidence that what the country needed was more austerity.

16

The Great Shame

FRANCO MARIA MALFATTI WAS an Italian politician who traced his lineage back to Philip of France, a rather brutal and avaricious thirteenth-century king.

Jim Tunney from Finglas was Fianna Fáil TD for Dublin North-West.

When they met, around May 1971, Malfatti was President of the European Commission (the position now held by José Manuel Barroso). He was steering the Commission planning the future integration of Europe. He would later become the Italian Minister for Finance.

Jim Tunney, a former teacher, at the age of fifty had been a TD for just two years.

At that time, the European Economic Community consisted of just West Germany, France, Italy, the Netherlands, Belgium and Luxembourg. For some time, Denmark, the UK and Ireland had been negotiating to join – which they would do eighteen months later.

As part of the negotiations, delegations were sent from the

applicant countries, to get to know EEC officials and their institutions. Such get-togethers aimed at creating meetings of minds, at which relationships could be formed and developed.

The London magazine *Private Eye* noted the visit of Tunney's delegation, and the fact that its members were hugely impressed by the trappings of the European bureaucracy:

> The climax of the Brussels visit was a meeting between
> the Irish delegation and Signor Franco Maria Malfatti,
> President of the European Commission. In the plush
> surroundings of the President's office, Mr Tunney did
> what he felt was expected of him. He asked for Signor
> Malfatti's autograph.

Anyone familiar with the style and behaviour of our political class, whether at home or in their dealings with the European Union, will recognize that undisguised mixture of pride and deference that characterizes Irish politicians: pride at having achieved a certain status, deference to those higher up the food chain.

Jim Tunney from Finglas was mixing with the European gentry. He was representing his country, playing a small part in an historic continental shift, the economic convergence of great nations – a movement that had been under way since shortly after the Second World War. It was a movement that promised great advances for his own little nation. And who wouldn't want a small keepsake of this moment? So Jim asked for Signor Malfatti's autograph.

Jim Tunney was intelligent and capable, but he lived within the suffocating world of Irish party politics, which is tribal, hierarchical, encouraging submissiveness to those above. Irish politics is a kiss-up, kick-down world. And, in the presence of a superior being, Jim made a display of submission.

One of the reasons we are now in terrible trouble is the nature of our political parties and their tenuous relationship with democracy. Another is the long-term attitude of deference towards the European bureaucracy.

For so many years, the EU was all about how much the politicians could negotiate. They got very good at smarming their way to Brussels and back. And much of the 'debate' about our relationship with the EU was about who could bring home the most cash while giving the least concessions. The EU wasn't being generous, it was smoothing out the single market. And, sometimes, Irish interests – whether agriculture, fisheries or industry – had to take one for the team.

Major developments were never debated publicly in political or economic terms. The Maastricht Treaty and the Growth and Stability Pact were discussed as technical measures which those nice folk in Europe needed to take to ensure the whole thing worked more efficiently. And we'd better go along with it, or they'd think less of us and we wouldn't be 'at the heart of Europe'.

After the 2008 crash, we found ourselves in a web of treaties and pacts that limited national sovereignty. 'Ah, sure, didn't we vote for that in 1992!'

After two years of the economy being undermined by austerity policies, the Great Shame arrived in late 2010.

That September, the reckless two-year blanket guarantee of the banks was to run out. The government renewed it, acting under strong pressure from the EU and, in particular, the European Central Bank. *No bank must be allowed to fail.*

For the sake of the Eurozone, the zombie Irish banks must be propped up, and pumped full of state money, so that they could pay back the billions they borrowed from German, French and UK banks. International investors were frantically jacking up interest rates on Irish state borrowing.

It became clear that the banks were in a worse state than anyone had thought, they'd need billions more, and the state was the fall guy. If the Irish state went bankrupt, any money the investors loaned to Ireland might not be repaid.

So, they pushed up interest rates. Up and up again, until by November 2010 the interest rates were so high the state couldn't afford to borrow.

These interest-rate rises, or bond yields, weren't a result of the recession in the real economy. Nor of any belief that the state was spending too much on social welfare, health or education. State spending was manageable. It had as collateral a sustainable economy, a skilled workforce that could create and sell goods and services, a strong consumer base and a proven record of exports. Whatever the strain on the state caused by falling Revenue receipts and rising unemployment, it wasn't government spending that threatened the solvency of the state.

It was the tens of billions the state was pissing away on zombie banks. Money thrown away. And no knowing how much more good money would be thrown after bad.

So, the Troika – the EU, ECB and IMF – arranged what they called a bail-out.

At this stage, behind the scenes, Brian Lenihan was subjected to ruthless pressure. Lenihan had been delighted when the IMF suggested to him that it was time the private bondholders took some pain. They had gambled with Seanie FitzPatrick and the rest of the careless bankers, and they lost. Tough luck: in the language of the finance business, it was time to burn the bondholders.

Believing the Irish citizens were about to be relieved of a debt of about €20 billion, Lenihan told the IMF's people: 'You are Ireland's salvation.'

At which point, the European Central Bank said no to the IMF suggestion.

In the week before the agreement, according to Lenihan's adviser, economist Alan Ahearne, the big issue was burning Anglo bondholders. Lenihan brought the senior members of the Troika together to discuss this.

Speaking to an Australian TV programme, *Four Corners*, Jürgen Stark, of the Executive Board of the ECB, explained why the ECB wanted bondholders protected. 'One has to consider the spill-over effect, to other market segments and to other countries, to other economies. And for that reason the Irish government was advised not to follow that path.'

'Advised' is not the word. The ECB was keeping Irish banks alive with cheap money (which citizens will have to repay). Letters arrived from the ECB's chairman, Jean Claude Trichet. Lenihan was left in no doubt: take on all the debt, pretend the bondholders' gambles didn't fail, or we collapse your banking system.

Jörg Asmussen of the ECB executive board told *Four Corners*: 'The very large Irish banking sector has linkages all over Europe. In the Eurozone, non-Eurozone countries – obviously the UK, but there's also a strong link across the Atlantic.'

So, as the Troika management discussed this, support for the ECB arrived in a conference call from the US Treasury Secretary, Tim Geithner. From the ECB to the US Treasury, all were agreed: put the private debt on the public bill.

The rationale is: protect bankers and bondholders. Only then can they rise again. And as they and their class prosper, ever more wealth will trickle down through the economy, to the rest of us.

To some, this is a harsh, ruthless and mad theory of how we should organize our affairs. To others, the natural order of things.

The 'bail-out' was a stitch-up.

Again, what matters is the flow of the money.

Billions, borrowed by the Troika on the money markets, flow into the Irish banks. That's the 'bail-out'. And a large amount of that money goes through the Irish banks to the German, French and UK banks. And from there to the bondholders who loaned money to the European banks. And the debts of Irish citizens grow by an equivalent amount.

As a *Business & Finance* magazine editorial later put it:

> This country took one for the euro-zone team when it
> absorbed banking losses through the Irish taxpayers.
> German banks were guaranteed every cent of their
> reckless lending.

In the course of bailing out the Eurozone banking system, our EU saviours borrowed the 'bail-out' cash on the money markets at about 3 per cent – and then charged the Irish state about 6 per cent. Our saviours were making as much from the deal as the private investors who loaned the money.

November 2010, as the Cowen government negotiated the terms on which the Troika would take over the running of the country, the *Irish Times* published an emotional editorial. 'Was it for this,' the editorial asked, that 'the men of 1916 died?'

The editorial spoke of 'the shame of it all', of how the 'desire to be a sovereign people runs like a seam through all the struggles of the last 200 years'. The newspaper felt awash with 'ignominy' at the loss of our 'self-determination'.

This reflected a genuine mood at some levels of society, where people spoke of shame, embarrassment and humiliation. Some likened it – incredibly – to the Germans marching into Paris in June 1940.

But many of us felt no shame, not having done anything shameful. As for self-determination, that depended on who the 'self' was.

For decades, a layer of well-off people had rather more self-determination than the rest of us. The party donors, the bankers, the builders, the bondholders, the lobbyists – and their servants in the professions and cheerleaders in the media – all had maximum self-determination. They directly influenced economic and social policy. They got precisely the set-up they wanted, and it crashed the country.

Now they and their hangers-on were weeping because they'd lost their status. No longer were they influencing major decisions over a round of golf or a meal in an expensive restaurant. The Troika representatives came, checked the books and went away, and never brought their golf clubs.

To the embarrassment of Official Ireland, a committee of the German Bundestag got into the habit of reading and discussing the Irish budget before it was revealed to the Oireachtas.

It was mostly a status thing that was being mourned. There was no policy change. The Troika's policies came from the same neo-liberal bible from which Irish politicians took their cue. Therefore, the outcome was more or less the same: austerity inflicted on the citizens, in an effort to revive the dead banks and infuse the entre-preneurial classes, here and abroad, with confidence.

The main difference was that the Troika technicians didn't have to listen to the entreaties of the bankers, builders and lobbyists.

The political class adapted quickly to the new regime. Ever vigilant to their place in the pecking order, Irish politicians quickly figure out which backs can be stabbed and which backsides must be kissed. They smiled and thanked 'our external friends' for their help.

In May of 2011, in an article in the *Irish Times*, economist Morgan Kelly revealed that in the midst of the 'bail-out' discussions six months earlier, the US Treasury Secretary had 'vetoed' the notion that Anglo bondholders could be burned, as Brian Lenihan and the IMF wanted. Kelly: 'The deal was torpedoed from an unexpected direction. At a conference call with the G7 finance ministers, the haircut was vetoed by US treasury secretary Timothy Geithner.'

Two weeks after Kelly's revelation, the new taoiseach, Enda Kenny, met with Geithner's boss, Barack Obama. And, a month later, the new Minister for Finance, Michael Noonan, met with Tim Geithner.

Face to face: the taoiseach tasked by the Troika with enforcing year after year of austerity; and the boss of the man who backed the deepening of Ireland's debts by €20 billion.

What did Kenny say to Obama about this?

We have his assurance that he simply didn't raise the matter. Not a goddamn word.

Face to face, a month later: the Minister for Finance tasked with deciding the depth of the cuts the citizens would suffer; and Tim Geithner, the man who believed that Irish citizens must pay the failed bets of international gamblers.

What did Noonan say to Geithner about this?

Briefing notes prepared for Geithner (acquired by RTÉ, through Freedom of Information) show that Geithner was warned that Noonan might raise the issue. Enda Kenny, the notes said, 'faced sharp domestic criticism when he acknowledged that he did not ask President Obama about your reported opposition during the President's visit to Dublin last month'.

So, Geithner was briefed on repulsing Noonan's questions about the twenty billion. He was ready, primed – there were five paragraphs in the briefing documents that reminded Geithner of who benefited from the decision to protect bondholders. Geithner was ready to answer Noonan.

How did it go?

Noonan funked it. Never raised the issue.

Not a goddamn word.

When the briefing document was much later released, the five paragraphs detailing the rationale behind Geithner's actions, reminding him who benefited, where the money went, were blacked out.

Noonan came out of the meeting with Geithner like a ten-year-old girl who had just shared a milkshake with Justin Bieber. He was impressed that Geithner had given him his personal phone numbers and told him to feel free to call if he needed advice.

In the best Irish political tradition of submissiveness to superior beings, neither Kenny nor Noonan felt it was their place to raise the issue of the €20 billion robbery of the Irish citizens.

Jim Tunney's little show of deference to Franco Maria Malfatti, all those years ago, was a harmless curtsy in comparison. We'll never know, of course, but some of us might conclude that, in circumstances where there were billions involved, Jim Tunney would have displayed more backbone.

17

The New Liberators

ON FRIDAY, 17 AUGUST 2012, perhaps in need of a rest after helping his granny celebrate her Diamond Jubilee, Prince Henry Charles Albert David of Wales set off with some male friends for Las Vegas. Commonly known as Prince Harry (of the House of Saxe-Coburg and Gotha, currently trading under the name House of Windsor), the young chap met a number of young women at the Wynn Hotel and took them up to his suite, where a game of strip billiards ensued. Before anyone could say, 'Nice shot, Your Royal Highness,' the inevitable phone-camera photos of the naked prince appeared on the internet.

Harry's granny's people advised the UK press not to publish the photos. Nervous about the continuing controversy over tabloid tactics, the newspapers studied the shots of the royal backside, bit their nails and let deadlines pass.

The Irish newspapers, too, held back. Using agency copy, papers in the UK and the *Irish Times* online primly reassured readers that, in the pictures, 'there is no suggestion that anything other than horseplay is going on between the royal and the unnamed woman'.

The *Star* had no such inhibitions. It immediately published the snaps and lambasted the other newspapers for failing to do so:

> The *Star* is the only newspaper that had the guts yesterday to defy the wishes of Britain's Queen Elizabeth and publish the pictures of Prince Harry in the nude. The other so-called Irish tabloids bent the knee to the British Monarchy . . .

And so on. Which was great fun, given that UK-based newspapers constantly go to some lengths in the Irish market to prove their Irishness. The *Star* trashed the 'pathetic British rags' that 'have the cheek to call themselves Irish'.

Then, the *Star* decided to claim for itself the role of carrying on the tradition of Pearse and MacDonagh, of Ceannt, Clarke and Plunkett: 'For God's sake, was it for this that the men and women of 1916 fought and died for Ireland's independence?'

If words mean anything (and, increasingly, in this bizarre little nation, they may not) these words reconfigure the definition of the struggle for Irish independence: our freedom is now defined by our right to publish snapshots of a foreign prince's arse. (Delighted with this success, the *Star* later made a further gesture of national sovereignty by printing snapshots of an English duchess's breasts, which got the paper into all kinds of trouble.)

We have to make allowances for a tabloid newspaper. It's an anything-goes commercial enterprise. However, when the taoiseach and his ministers rewrite the definition of Irish independence and national sovereignty, the consequences are more serious.

In the second week of May 2011, just weeks in office, Cabinet minister Pat Rabbitte defined the government's 'over-riding national objective'. It is to 'restore the independence of the country and wave goodbye to the ECB'.

A month later, Taoiseach Enda Kenny announced that he wanted to 'wave goodbye to the IMF'. As is his style, the taoiseach took to using the phrase repeatedly. Sometimes it was rejigged as 'wave goodbye to Ajai Chopra', the senior IMF representative.

Then, Tánaiste Eamon Gilmore began announcing that he wanted as quickly as possible to 'say goodbye to the IMF'.

This chorus of politicians singing from the same hymn sheet was no coincidence.

In November 2010, Fianna Fáil effectively handed the country over to what we were supposed to call 'our external partners'. The Great Shame was followed by a perceptible rise in indignant nationalistic feeling.

On being elected four months later, Enda Kenny and Eamon Gilmore saw how easy it would be to capitalize on that emotion. Their medium-term political strategy became obvious. It's political in the party sense, in the electoral sense. It is to 'restore the independence of the country' and 'wave goodbye' to the symbol of outsider rule.

For decades, Fianna Fáil wrapped the green flag around themselves. They were the people who claimed to embody the Spirit of the Nation. The Blueshirt Fine Gaelers and the pinko Labour comrades had long been cast as vaguely less than Irish. The upstart Sinn Féin still had a whiff of Semtex about it, and it would take a long time to wash that away.

Through decade after decade, Fianna Fáil were the sea-green incorruptibles – until their political, and in some cases personal, corruption became obvious even to their fans. And then their government became the local office of the Troika, a Vichy regime taking orders from abroad.

Now, with Fianna Fáil on the ropes, the way was open for Fine Gael and Labour to snatch up that fallen green flag and wrap it around themselves, once and for all killing off the Fianna Fáil claim to more fully represent the national spirit.

And, doing it just in time for the 1916 centenary. Do it right, and they might permanently make Fianna Fáil an also-ran.

It's not hard to see what they're up to.

Everything the government does is ostentatiously geared towards 'waving goodbye to the IMF', and 'restoring independence'. Enda Kenny, December 2011: 'I want to be the taoiseach who returns Ireland's economic sovereignty.'

The damage done to Fianna Fáil was so great that their rivals see a world of possibilities. Perhaps Fine Gael and Labour have notions of facing off at the next election as potential government and opposition, with Fianna Fáil for evermore reduced to a husk.

So, what's wrong with that?

What's wrong with waving goodbye to the Troika?

What's wrong with restoring the independence of the country?

What's wrong, for that matter, with killing off Fianna Fáil?

If Kenny and Gilmore manage to get rid of the Troika and restore sovereignty, won't they be the New Liberators, the Pearse and Collins of their day? As it happens, in August 2012, Enda Kenny gave a speech at the site of the ambush at Béal na mBláth in which Michael Collins was killed. He made a very deliberate pitch to be seen as the inheritor of the mantle of Collins:

> In recent days, I have been thinking a lot about Michael
> Collins . . . with the destiny of a nation on his shoulders
> . . . we are again, as Collins did, having to build, to
> rebuild, our economy and restructure our institutions . . .
> just as Collins was undeterred by the dire financial straits
> in which Ireland found itself in the 1920s, the government
> I lead is equally determined . . .

In keeping with Collins's ambition, mental force and
high ideals . . . the government is approaching our task of
national recovery with the passion and determination and
zeal that Collins would have applied . . . Michael Collins
wrote: Give us back our country, to live in, to grow in, to
love. These aspirations reflect my own. We have no time
to waste.

Okay, there's a bit of juvenile posing going on, Enda throwing
Michael Collins shapes. But, what matter if Enda is trying to find a
place in history? What matter, as long as we take 'back our country'
and 'wave goodbye to the IMF'?

The problem is:

Facing the worst economic crisis in the history of the state, the
government hasn't had an economic policy. It has a political policy
that centres on party advancement: finish off Fianna Fáil. In so far
as the government has had any economic aims, it was a crude hope
that austerity would come close to balancing the books. And that,
with an appropriate amount of bowing and scraping and pleading,
would get a concession on debt, to ease the burden of taking on
bankers' debts.

In order to advance the party-political objectives, the government had no wider political strategy, other than subservience.
Whatever the Troika wanted the Troika would get. Welfare cuts,
tax increases, sales of state assets, a measure inserted into the constitution – it didn't matter. Some might argue that these policies
would do long-term damage to the country – it didn't matter.

The government parties, in pursuit of their own political
ambitions, were ready to make any concession, engage in any act of
deference they judged necessary. Meet the targets, get a pat on the
head from the Troika, eventually the money markets would let us
back in to borrow – and we would be free, our sovereignty regained.

And Fianna Fáil would be history.

Having opposed mindless subservience to the Troika when Fianna Fáil was in office, Fine Gael and Labour now adopted the same strategy.

They do not, of course, see themselves as self-serving. They see themselves as striving to end the Great Shame, to free the people. They see their political goal and the welfare of the people as one. Just as Fianna Fáil believed for all those years that the interests of the people were best served by having Fianna Fáil in government – and that justified whatever they did to ensure that, including taking dodgy donations and pandering to the interests of those who funded the party.

But does it matter what this government's motives are? Wouldn't it be great to see the back of that Troika shower?

To 'wave goodbye to the IMF' now redefines political progress.

Not the rate of unemployment.

Not the state of the economy.

Not the level of growth.

Not the welfare of the old, the young and the sick.

Not the state of the hospitals.

Not the effects on the education of the next generation.

The measure of all things is the party-political advantage to be gained from 'waving goodbye to the IMF'.

It's all about making sure that Enda Kenny and Eamon Gilmore get to wave their fists in the air and crown themselves the New Liberators. It's all about kicking Fianna Fáil when it's down, and kicking it so hard that it never gets up again.

It's not as though 'waving goodbye to the IMF' will change anything.

The same policy of austerity will continue into the far distance. Since the cost of borrowing will be higher, the austerity may well be deeper. Deals on debt reduce the scale by which the citizens are being mugged, but the government continues to rack up huge debts in our name, to bail out the dead banks. We'll be paying off interest and capital a generation from now.

Meanwhile, if Michael Noonan is unsure of what to do – well, he has a new friend. Here's what he said, in an RTÉ interview, after his meeting in Washington with Tim Geithner, the man who, in Morgan Kelly's opinion, is said to have 'vetoed' the IMF suggestion that Anglo bondholders should be forced to take their losses:

> We left each other on the basis that I could ring him any
> time on his personal telephone numbers . . . if events went
> dramatically wrong some time in Europe and we needed
> an outside perspective – well, I have someone who's going
> to give it to me, now.

The Minister for Finance is grateful to be able to consult, in matters of international finance, a man whose job it is to place US interests above those of Irish citizens.

18

The Great War Against Ourselves

WHEN KATHLEEN MCLAUGHLIN WON €2.6 million in the Lotto before Christmas 2011, the 78-year-old Donegal woman was pleased but not overexcited. 'If it had come forty years ago it would have been better use for me than getting it now.'

Her big purchase was a sofa. 'I hate travelling,' she told the *Irish Independent*. 'I hate planes and I don't do well on boats, so I'm happy enough to enjoy myself at home.'

With seven children and twenty-eight grandchildren, she was now in a position to help a lot of people. She paid off her children's mortgages, for instance. She sounds like a happy, decent person, who wouldn't be derailed by sudden wealth. 'I have my bingo, and I just love going to that and meeting my friends.'

The state stopped her pension.

It was a non-contributory pension, so it was means tested. Kathleen didn't make a fuss about it; she has enough now to see her through her days. But it's the sheer meanness that matters. At seventy-eight, she enjoyed the status of an elder, receiving back a portion of the monies she paid in taxes. Decade after decade, every time she bought something – a scarf or a biscuit, a box of matches or a tin of polish – she was setting a little tax aside for her future. Now, the lackeys of austerity are everywhere, patting us down, checking our wallets, seeking ways to scrape excess butter off our bread.

Four years after the bankers, developers and politicians crashed the country, it's become a very mean place. And dangerous. There's a big bill to pay – billions borrowed and squandered – and there's a pretence that there's nowhere else to get the money but from the pockets of the low- and medium-paid. Despite the evidence of our eyes, we must believe that those who crashed the country are broke.

Most of all, the austerity fetish disguises the basic economics of the strategy: to drive down aggregate demand, to drive up unemployment, and thus force down wages. Result: cheaper and more flexible labour, which leads to bigger profits; and the Austerity Hawks believe that will attract investment and spur recovery.

That's what it says in their dogma. And if it works they get recovery at the expense of those on average wages. If it doesn't work – well, more austerity. In the old phrase attributed to disciplinarians in the pre-war Japanese navy: 'The beatings will continue until morale improves.'

Meanwhile, every cent off the deficit brings us closer to the day we 'wave goodbye to the IMF', and isn't that worth going hungry for?

May 2012, in a primary school in Cork, a seven-year-old collapsed. A doctor was called, then social services; the verdict was 'severe under-nutrition'. The child's mother had an empty fridge on Wednesdays; when she got the social welfare on Thursdays, she could buy food.

Under pressure to pay off debts, with new charges and reduced income, some people are on a knife edge. In a 2004 survey, 17 per cent of children said they went to bed hungry. For the same survey in 2010, the figure was 21 per cent – one in five.

St Vincent de Paul workers tell of parents doing without food so their kids can eat. Brendan Dempsey of the Cork branch told the *Irish Examiner*: 'Two or three years ago we were being asked for shoes or help with the rent. Now we are simply being asked for food. The politicians are living with their heads in the clouds.'

The Great War against Ourselves is accompanied by claims that 'the most vulnerable' will be protected. The most vulnerable are, by definition, those least able to resist. Politicians on an austerity drive are like any other bullies. They pick on those least likely to kick back.

Which is why the old and infirm, desperately in need of a small measure of support, were targeted. There is a multitude of small things that can be beyond any of us when we are ill or in our final days, infirmities that degrade the quality of the hours in a day, things that make the house inhospitable, difficult to live in. You're too infirm to clean properly, so you are ashamed to ask someone round for a chat.

One hour a week from a home help can change that. It can make a life easier, brighter, more open.

Fifty-two hours a year, a home help may come and clean, prepare a meal, post a letter, open a window, sit and chat, fix something or fetch something, change a fuse, have a proper search for the glasses you've misplaced and without which you can't watch television. Such work is not highly paid, and it makes the difference between dignity and humiliation. A clean floor and a cardigan searched for and found, a room tidied, may make the difference between being alone and feeling ready to invite an old friend around. There comes a time, for all of us, when such things matter deeply. And one hour a week can make that difference.

So, the politicians decided to save money by cutting 600,000 hours of home help per year. Six hundred thousand small mercies sacrificed on the altar of austerity.

Severely disabled people, threatened with the loss of personal assistants, without whom they cannot function – work, move about, achieve a measure of independence – besieged Leinster House. Some sat outside all night in their wheelchairs, until they got a promise in writing that the threat of such cuts would be rescinded. The severity of their circumstances worked for them; even some politicians were aghast at the thought of picking the pockets of these people.

They have cut support for rape victims.

They have cut support for hospices.

They have cut support for special-needs children.

They have cut suicide-prevention resources.

Programmes that can make the difference between a kid finishing school or dropping out are cut back.

Over here, a politician making a passionate speech about the importance of education, about how this country will prosper because of the great system of education that blah, blah, blah.

Over there, teaching posts ripped out of rural Ireland.

Over here, a politician talking about how the children of the nation blah, blah, blah.

Around the corner, parents of children with autism and special needs wonder how they're going to hold things together without the domiciliary-care allowance.

A year into the crisis, in September 2009, a banker called Michael Soden appeared on TV3's *Tonight with Vincent Browne*. There was a woman on the programme who said she feared cuts to lone-parent allowances in the budget coming in December.

'With all due respect,' said Mr Soden, 'lone parents should —'

And he paused. Then continued, 'I'm sorry. I'm on the other side.'

Usually, people from the elite layers play the 'we're all equal' game. Mr Soden, however, was honest.

'I don't think that society should be carrying the burden. That's just a political —' Mr Soden paused again. 'You've got a social status; I have one,' he said.

Vincent Browne said, 'Michael, you can't believe that.'

'I can,' said Soden.

The *Irish Examiner* asked him to expand on his views: 'Mr Soden said that if people choose the single-parent-family life they have to be responsible for themselves and not depend on the state.'

Now, there are several ways to look at this. The notion of a former CEO of the Bank of Ireland urging people to 'be responsible' and 'not depend on the state', given the amount of public money squandered on bailing out that bank, is quite amusing.

It could be a brave statement of a class warrior. It could be Mr Soden believes that the state should not subsidize the rearing of the children of unmarried women, that it should instead confine its social welfare to the care and sustenance of bankers and their bedraggled institutions. By the way, when Mr Soden had to resign from the Bank of Ireland in 2004 he got a €2.3 million send-off. Plus €400,000 into his pension pot.

Sixty per cent of single parents work, and 20 per cent more are in training or education. These are people who struggle to give their kid a decent start and who do it with the barest of support. Every child who gets a decent start is an asset to this nation.

In October 2010, three days after the government appointed him to the Central Bank Commission, Mr Soden suggested that public servants should be made to work an extra half-day a week.

The Fianna Fáil/Green government had been burned badly when they had followed Seanie FitzPatrick's urging to hit pensioners' medical cards. The pensioners caused a big row and the government took a hiding. So, although that government respected

Mr Soden's views, it kept its hands off the lone-parent payment.

However, the incoming Fine Gael/Labour people were just as respectful of Mr Soden. And they felt there might be something worth cutting in the lone-parent area. The one-parent-family payment stops when the child reaches eighteen. In 2011, Enda Kenny's people decided to reduce that to fourteen, in stages, by 2016.

Then, as though afraid that such a move might look bad in the centenary of the 1916 Rising, they brought it forward to 2015.

Then, shortly before Christmas 2011, they decided they should stop the payment when the child reaches seven.

Mr Soden also had a solution for the stagnant economy. NAMA should act to kick-start the property market, he told Newstalk FM in August 2012. If you woke up to find the property section of the newspapers reporting a 10 per cent increase in property prices, he said, 'the wonderful factor of greed would re-enter the marketplace, and you would find that there is a turn in the marketplace'.

As the Austerity Hawks pounded the life out of the economy, a banker held in great esteem by Official Ireland called for the encouragement of 'the wonderful factor of greed'. Mr Soden, in his blunt way, was honestly stating what too many members of the elites lack the courage to say – that greed is at the heart of their philosophy: greed is good, inequality is dynamic.

This philosophy was taught in business schools, where students heard of the delights of trickle-down economics and the invisible hand of the free market. And, even after free-market extremism crashed one economy after another, all they could do was keep pushing the same buttons.

In the real world, nurses called for the opening of 1,300 acute hospital beds, to break the logjam that slows everything right through the system and leads to patients being stuck for hours and days on trolleys. They'd been calling for that for years, while consultants claim that overcrowding creates 'a daily risk to patient safety'.

It's not just frustrating to have to wait six hours untreated in A&E; after that time, the chances increase of something serious developing. And 35 per cent of patients go beyond that time. The record measured time waiting for a bed is 137 hours – almost six days.

Hospitals, desperate to meet targets set by accountants – not medical targets, management theory targets – are culling lists, to see if they can reject patients on the basis that they're 'outside the catchment area'. People are shuffled from one list to another, as medical staff try to work under the strictures set by the Austerity Hawks.

If targets aren't met, fines are imposed on the hospital. Because everyone knows that taking money away from hospitals that were already underfunded is a great way to improve our health.

It's as if someone with a diploma in railroad scheduling has been hired to supervise the running of hospitals – using techniques picked up from a book of neoliberal management techniques – and has been given powers that can further damage the ability of the hospital staff to do their jobs.

It's almost as though, for these people, none of this is happening in the real world. It's as though these are figures on a spreadsheet, not people in pain and in danger.

Everyone knows there are problems in hospitals and schools that could be put right with better organization. That's not what this is about. This is about taking money away from the public realm, cutting the social wage, driving down one side of the balance sheet. And, at precisely the same time, running up huge debts by unconditionally channelling free money to the finance business.

Not that these two happenings are in any way related.

On RTÉ News, Joe Little reported on a woman who looked after her mother, who needed incontinence pads. The woman was required to keep a 'bladder report chart', measuring the intake of liquids and the output, to see if savings could be made on the number of incontinence pads used. In April 2012, the HSE instructed nursing homes to save money by giving each patient one fewer incontinence pad per day. The HSE later withdrew this instruction.

Stalwarts of Official Ireland, such as the employer lobbyists IBEC, demanded cuts in the staffing of the public service, using the 'share the pain' mantra. The huge salaries and obscene pensions given to civil-service mandarins were used to attack the public sector, as though all public servants were paid a fortune.

Oddly enough, if you suppress the spending power of a large section of the workforce – the public service – they will spend less, hitting jobs in the private sector. In its attacks on the public sector, IBEC was attacking its own members' customer base.

Employment forced down, virtually the entire workforce unsettled and fearful for its future, spending less, depressing the economy. And they wondered why the economy remained flatlined.

Of course, it wasn't all bad news.

19

And the Winner is . . .

E CONOMISTS AND ECONOMIC ANALYSTS use language that couldn't be termed pretty – or even accessible. It often seems as though they're deliberately cloaking their information in some obscure dialect distantly related to the language the rest of us use. Probably it's just a bad habit they develop by too often limiting their conversation to others of their kind.

Example: in March 2012 the Central Statistics Office (CSO) released a review of incomes and concluded that between 2009 and 2010 there was 'an uneven distribution of the percentage change in equivalised disposable income across the deciles'.

To translate:

The CSO divides us into ten income groups. We can see this in a chart on the next page.

On the far left of the chart, the lowest earning. Then, eight other groups to the right of them; and then, on the far right, the highest paid. (The people putting their names down for those expensive handbags in Brown Thomas.)

After all the demands that we 'share the pain' equally, we find

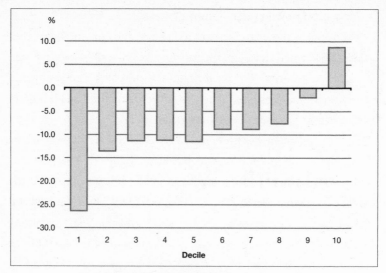

**Percentage change in equivalized disposable
household income by decile SILC 2010**

that the lowest paid took a 26 per cent hit in their disposable income
in 2010.

In the middle of the chart, those in the middle-earning group
took about a 12 per cent cut.

And, over on the right, with the expensive handbags, those in
the highest-earning group had an 8 per cent increase in disposable
income.

Throughout the boom, it had been the habit of layers of people
– bankers, politicians, academics, consultants, top civil servants,
company executives, etc. – to ensure they were paid rock-star
wages. Plus grandiose pensions, extravagant share options and loot
without limit.

And the support groups below them, their cheerleaders and
camp followers, were rewarded with far greater than average pay.
The justification of such rewards – when they bother with justification – is: we're worth it. It's not about the value of the work they do,
it's about their social status.

Now, a very obvious fact jumps up here.

Who among these layers of exalted ones could convincingly claim to have performed so well in their given tasks that they were entitled to such vast rewards? The performance of the elites plainly failed to justify such bounties. Even those who performed adequately were overpaid for no reason other than social position.

And the payment was immense. A range of researchers – Michael Taft, the Think-tank for Action on Social Change (TASC), Peadar Kirby, Mary Murphy, etc. – have assembled evidence on pay. At the height of the boom, from 2005 to 2007, pay of CEOs of state-owned and private companies rose on average by 40 per cent, averaging €1.1 million. In the two years to 2009, covering the crash of the economy and the onset of austerity, their average pay went up by 46 per cent, to €1.6 million.

A layer of managerial and professional types dominate the top 0.5 per cent of the population; on average, they have an income of at least €600,000. During the Celtic Bubble, much of the running was made by these people gambling on the property market. Private hospitals, hotels, car parks, apartment blocks, housing estates – nothing to do with health, tourism, transport or housing; all driven by tax breaks and speculation. What Mr Michael Soden referred to as 'the wonderful factor of greed'.

And the global evidence of the wonderful factor of greed was, indeed, impressive. The Tax Justice Network published research in 2012 which showed that, globally, at least $21 trillion is hidden offshore by the rich, in secret tax havens. This isn't primarily tax-evasion money, it is the excess rewards accumulated by the global elites. Some tax evasion, no doubt, and much moved away via aggressive but legal tax-avoidance schemes. All of it the accumulation from a system that vastly over-rewards the top layers of society – that diverts immense wealth into tax havens, where it stays, stagnant, non-productive.

Under the austerity regime, now that the system has crashed, the greatest burden of saving the economy is borne by people on lower and medium incomes.

Very many of those who benefited most from the Celtic Bubble – and here we're talking about the highly paid bankers, politicians, academics, consultants, top civil servants, company executives – are surrounded by sycophants who praise them endlessly, and scapegoats who can be sacrificed when necessary. Even if they performed superbly, they would still be vastly overpaid. Given their record, the myth of some kind of ratio between talent and performance is in tatters.

If truck drivers, cleaners, book keepers, train drivers, bank clerks, shop assistants and factory workers performed to the same low standards, the country would grind to a halt.

Yet this blatant truth hasn't stopped the elites demanding that they keep their premium salaries and perks. Instead, they have taken it for granted that any end to the crisis is conditional on all dysfunctional hierarchies and habits, and the structural inequalities they breed, being maintained.

There might be token concessions, to show that they share our pain, but the structure of vast and damaging inequality of income and wealth is non-negotiable.

Bankers, for instance, complain about a pay limit of half a million euro a year. Some of them have managed to breach that limit. The logic was that if they didn't get such rewards they would take their talents elsewhere. It would be nice to be a fly on the wall at an interview anywhere on the planet where one of those people was applying for a job.

'And what did you do last?'

'I made the Irish banking system what it is today.'

The culture of rock-star rewards saturates the highest-paid layers of the country. Here's Michael Murphy, president of University College Cork (salary €232,000), quoted in the *Irish Examiner*: 'When you take on a job as a university head, you have an anticipation that there will be a certain salary going with it. You will have bought the house, you will have got the mortgage, which will be bigger than the one from, you know (before).'

One has one's expectations, hasn't one?

And the apologists for the elites warn that unless they are vastly rewarded they might leave the country and deprive us of their talents. Well, off you go, then. The graveyards are full of indispensable people.

And the country is full of ambitious, capable young people and there are few jobs we can't fill from their ranks.

There are some jobs, highly technical, which require vast experience and specialized knowledge, and these can be done by few people, and they may demand a premium. Most of the top jobs are overpaid solely because of what Michael Soden called his 'social status'.

Some demand that we must abandon pay limits so we can attract Irish people from abroad to run the public service – and they couldn't be expected to accept a measly €200,000. To ask them to do so, the *Irish Independent* concluded, with its tongue entirely absent from its cheek, would be 'a strain on patriotism if ever there was one'.

In the run-up to the centenary of 1916, we're inventing some bizarre definitions of patriotism – accepting a €200,000 per annum job.

Taoiseach Enda Kenny ostentatiously cut his salary to a mere €200,000 a year (plus car and driver and a long list of perks). This left him at a rate just €28,000 a year more than British Prime Minister David Cameron (who earns the equivalent of €172,000).

Ministerial pay cuts followed. Now, people like Minister for Finance Michael Noonan earn a belittling €169,000 a year. Mr

Noonan's equivalent in the USA, his old buddy US Treasury Secretary Tim Geithner, earns the US dollar equivalent of €150,400.

When the Governor of the Central Bank, Professor Patrick Honohan, took a patriotic pay cut, his salary was reduced to €276,000. His US equivalent, Ben Bernanke, Chairman of the Federal Reserve, is on the equivalent of €157,000.

In July 2011, on being promoted to Chief Justice, Supreme Court Judge Susan Denham waived a €38,000 pay increase. Very laudable, given that many hard-working Irish people earn considerably less than €38,000. The *Irish Independent* published a piece noting that the US Chief Justice gets the dollar equivalent of €154,000. In Ireland, it's €296,000.

And, the *Independent* said, a senior judge in Ireland is paid about two and a half times what an equivalent judge earns in France.

The top layers of the Irish private sector insist on their bloated pay packets, even as they wield the axe against the blind, the sick and the low- and medium-paid.

These people seem to have no sense of irony. Take John Bruton, former taoiseach. In August 2011 he issued a ringing call for citizens to reject 'a living standard they had not earned'. In this age of austerity, there must be an end to 'restrictive practices and padded costs'.

Bruton had a lucrative career after he quit the Dáil in October 2004. He was appointed to a number of EU positions, each of which we can conclude was well paid. He then moved to the private sector as a mouthpiece for the finance industry based in the IFSC, which we might imagine is not a minimum-wage gig.

Google his name and the word 'speakers' and you'll find a number of websites advertising his charms as a speaker: 'helped transform the Irish economy into the Celtic Tiger, one of the fastest growing economies in the world . . . has met with the current President and former Presidents of the United States . . . A dynamic visionary,

Ambassador John Bruton has held the fate of European countries in his hands . . . '

And that won't come cheap.

On top of all this, while urging ever greater austerity on the mugs, Mr Bruton was drawing a state pension. What work did Mr Bruton do to justify this pension?

Bruton was Fine Gael leader when the Fianna Fáil/Labour government collapsed in 1994. Labour switched sides and went into a coalition with Fine Gael. Bruton became taoiseach without an election. When he had to go before the electorate three years later, he was kicked out.

He was taoiseach for two and a half years. It would be nice to be able to report that at any time after he left the job in 1997 the populace sighed and said, 'Oh, if only we had John back things would be so much better.' In truth, he kept the seat warm after Albert Reynolds and before Bertie Ahern.

In the 1980s, for a total of nineteen months, Bruton was Minister for Finance. He was also employed in Industry and Trade, and he was a TD. For all this work he was very well paid.

Like most of us, on reaching retirement age, Mr Bruton would no doubt be due a modest pension. As a politician, leaving politics at the age of fifty-seven, to take on other well-paying jobs, he drew a pension immediately. That pension, at the time he lectured us on the benefits of austerity, was €138,000 a year, three times the size of the wage packet of most of the citizens.

In memory of his well-paid work as a politician, he was now on a pension of €2,650 a week.

He was asked by the *Irish Independent*, when he urged austerity on the rest of us, if he would waive that pension. After all, he'd been employed through the years since leaving politics, and was in a well-paid job. He said no.

(Phil Hogan, the Kenny/Gilmore minister with the job of

enforcing various austerity charges, was asked in 2009 if he'd take a pay cut – and he gave the answer he wouldn't accept from those he was strong-arming: 'No. My personal circumstances don't allow that at the moment.')

In John Bruton's 2011 demands for austerity he warned the people of Europe that 'prosperity is not a birthright'. He told us that 'none of us can solve our problems on the back of someone else's sacrifice'.

Not that there's anything unique about John Bruton. This has become the norm in politics.

20

The Laws of Distraction

FOR ALL THEIR VAST rewards, Official Ireland can't honestly claim that their semi-religious theories of austerity politics are working.

Not here, not across Europe.

Still the Austerity Hawks push on.

Of course, they can't very well announce creative destruction as a policy. They continue to wear their sad faces when someone mentions unemployment. But it's quite clear that there is not now and has not been since the start of the crisis, and there will never be, a serious attempt to cut unemployment.

One major reason they get away with this is that they get to set the question, and the media doesn't challenge them. If the question is how to save the banks, it follows that you should give the banks an unconditional guarantee. If the question is how to meet Troika targets, how to save the euro, how to please the ECB, you cut services and impose charges on citizens. If the question is how you do this without causing real pain to the top layers, the alleged 'wealth creators' who destroyed the country's wealth – well, you ask them to contribute as much as won't distress them too much, and collect the rest by screwing those on average wages, the young, the sick and the disabled.

Another reason they get away with it is their well-honed ability to distract the rest of us into cul-de-sacs. Distract and divert, divide and rule.

Examples.

Rural dwellers mounted a determined campaign against septic-tank charges. They dubbed it 'the shit tax' and protests featured a man sitting on a toilet bowl, being pushed along by his mates. It was an energetic, effective campaign. Had that campaign been pitched as one of a number of protests against the consequences of austerity, reaching out to other protesters, it could have been stronger, it could have affected policy. Instead, it won concessions – and the Austerity Hawks plot to do better next time.

Inevitably, instead of seeing the protest as part of a wider resistance, someone used the Jackeen card. The campaign took on an anti-Dublin tinge, with the claim that them lousers up in Dublin were getting away with murder and piling all the charges on the poor rural dwellers. Something that quite obviously isn't true.

Here, for instance, is the most vocal of the protesters, Mattie McGrath TD (a Fianna Fáil politician from 1999 until he announced he was quitting the party a month before the 2011 general election. McGrath held on to his seat, while Fianna Fáilers fell like nettles before a scythe).

The septic-tank charge, he said, was 'another attack on rural dwellers as it seeks to penalize them with potentially crippling costs while urban dwellers will bear no cost and are protected by the tax payer'.

In Dublin, during any campaign against an equivalent charge, you could always rely on someone to have a go at them lousers down the country who won't pull their weight.

When resistance campaigns embarrass politicians and they back off, the austerity policies are ostentatiously adjusted to give a little – and quietly rejigged to take more from the same people under another heading. When we're divided, we can be used against each other, with advantages conceded flamboyantly and taken back quietly.

The notion that either city dwellers or rural dwellers are getting rich off the back of someone else's sacrifices is nonsense. Both are victims. The country is so small you could throw a stone from one side of it to the other. Campaigns on all sides would benefit from solidarity.

The factory worker and the country labourer have more in common than divides them. They are both targets for those who ran the country into the ground. However, in a country of tribes and clans, party loyalties and local obsessions, it's very easy to drive a wedge between them.

And, in too many instances, when people dig their heels in against some part of the austerity regime, it's pitched as being singularly unfair – and they point fingers at others who are supposedly more deserving of suffering. Don't cut me, cut my neighbour.

This is encouraged at every opportunity. *Look over there! Look at that guy! Get angry at him!* Don't look behind the curtain, let us do our work, let the recession do its work, don't interfere in what we're doing – stay angry at something else.

Distract and divert is used to pitch PAYE workers against the self-employed. The Irish-born against immigrants (when they come here they're 'illegal'; when our lads turn up in Boston they're merely 'undocumented'). Students versus workers. And vice versa. Private sector against public.

Kicking public-sector workers has become a regular hobby among the Austerity Hawks in the media. The Croke Park Agreement is routinely described in terms usually reserved for drug dealers and paedophiles. Take the fury directed at the €75 million cost of public-sector allowances – most of them legitimate. Michael Taft writes of the effect of that €75 million on the deficit, as a percentage of GDP: 0.032136. He compares this with the lack of rage at the effects of austerity.

'Yet,' writes Taft, 'over the last six months 1,200 jobs are being lost a week while €899 million has been wiped off domestic demand resulting in weakening public finances and even more misery in society.' Taft accurately characterizes this diversion as 'chasing mice while the elephants destroy the house'.

Distract and divert is used to blackguard the unemployed. The lazy buggers get more on the dole than at work, we're told. Not true, says the ESRI, for 96 per cent of the unemployed. In pursuit of the other four per cent, a policy of 'labour activation' makes the unemployed jump through hoops. At the bottom of this nonsense is the premise that there are hundreds of thousands of jobs just waiting to be filled.

Distract and divert is used, very cynically, to denigrate other countries in trouble. We were pushed into further developer and bank bail-outs by warnings that Iceland had destroyed itself by refusing to take on banker debt. And if we didn't do as we were told, we'd end up like Iceland.

How did that work out? By just about any measure – unemployment (half ours), debt, bank lending, domestic demand, they did okay. As economist Paul Krugman put it: 'Ireland did everything it was supposed to; nobody would describe it as "healing". Iceland broke all the rules, and things are not too bad.'

Michael Noonan spent much of 2011 sneering at Greece, threatening at one point to get T-shirts made with a slogan announcing we weren't like Greece. At a time when solidarity between countries in trouble could have influenced the disastrous ECB blundering, our leaders chose division.

Worse, they accepted the implication that the crisis arose from some kind of moral failure on the behalf of some countries. The implication was that other countries were more industrious, not lazy, more morally upright.

As it happens, the Greeks work over forty-two hours a week, the Germans fewer than thirty-six. The euro crisis isn't about moral flaws, it's about mismanaged interest rates, flows of capital and uneven trade balances and accumulation. It's about a banking system that took advantage of these factors to run up unsustainable levels of credit – in accordance with the economic theories of idiots – and crashed the lot.

When they're not pitching employed against unemployed, Irish against Greeks, they're trying to pitch young against old. The young are told the old are sitting back on cushions of cash – that there's 'massive intergenerational inequity'. Let's slash their benefits.

Meanwhile, the old are told excessive numbers of the young are living the high life on student grants. Set them one against the other, all the easier to cut the benefits to both.

The number of tip-offs on 'welfare fraud' went from 6,429 in 2009 to 16,920 in 2011. Those are not proven cases of welfare fraud; they are cases of neighbours, former work colleagues and casual strangers who have a hunch that someone is doing nixers while on the dole. Someone else has a boyfriend staying over while she's claiming a single-parent allowance. Such suspicions may or may not be well founded, but they all go on the books as tip-offs.

Before we go any further, obviously social-welfare fraud is a crime, as is any type of fraud. Is it a problem in Ireland? There are examples, every now and then, of some greedy gouger caught using several identities to steal benefits. To read all the stuff about tip-offs and crackdowns, ministers getting tough, neighbours ratting out the guy next door, you'd be justified in concluding that fraud is at epidemic levels. The bulletin of the Oireachtas Library and Research

Service, in a 2011 document titled 'Tackling Social Welfare Fraud', says: 'The Department of Social Protection in Ireland estimates that the level of fraud and error in the social welfare system ranges between 2.4–4.4% of total annual welfare expenditure.'

This is an estimate. Not of fraud, but of 'over-payments'. These figures include both error and fraud. And since experience suggests that 69 per cent of the total is error, we're looking at a fraud rate of about 1 per cent. That's the international norm.

The Comptroller and Auditor General estimated the cost of fraud in 2010 as €25.9 million. A lot of money – and no one should steal from the rest of us – but a tiny part of the budget. There are substantial controls, and they work. Whenever this is made an issue – usually with inflated claims of €600 million in savings, as ministers 'crack down' on fraud – it's a deliberate diversion. It uses the usual campaign of media leaks, half-truths and exaggerations designed to get us angry at the small number of fraudsters – it's a handy distraction from what's going on.

But aren't there real disparities in the ways we're all being hit, with some taking more of a hiding than others?

Of course. They take from us what they can manage, depending on circumstance. Sometimes one group of us gets hit harder than others; sometimes another group fights back and wins concessions. Making links between such groups could benefit all – instead, too often such differences are exploited to set one group against another.

Public-sector workers do earn more than private-sector workers: one piece of research put the respective average wages at €50,000 and €40,000. And there's a good reason for that, even leaving aside levels of qualifications. Most public-sector jobs are within established institutions, long unionized, and they get the proper rate for the job. Within the private sector, there are conscientious employers and there are economic thugs – people who see workers as disposable units, to be plugged in and discarded in accordance with profit trends.

Leave aside the fact that cutting public-sector income will cost private-sector jobs; leave aside all the cartoon business-speak about rugged individualists versus mollycoddled public servants. What would most of us prefer? To have a relatively secure job, with a decent wage, or to live according to the whims of a self-described 'entrepreneur' who treats staff and customers with equal venom?

Every secure job, with a fair wage and conditions, is a bonus to all of us. It stabilizes the economy. In the aggregate, such jobs stimulate the economy, circulate wealth, create other jobs.

Every sweat-shop job, with buttons wages and insecure conditions, diminishes us all. The enterprise exists to exploit cheap labour, to undermine competitors, to abuse state facilities, to make a quick buck and move on.

There are, of course, a variety of different kinds of jobs in between these two. There's nothing intrinsically good or bad about public or private sector in themselves; they are ways of doing things that have developed over a long time, each with its strengths and weaknesses.

What matters is that wherever we are, in public or private sector, under pressure from a government that's trying to maintain a failing neoliberal way of doing things, protecting the rich and treating the banks as a measure of our society, they use our differences to divide, isolate and defeat us. And they've been doing so deliberately, regardless of the long-term social effects. It's as though they see true debate as a luxury we can't afford. Their austerity propaganda is relentless; they no longer even pretend to explain policy truthfully and argue democratically.

21

How Democracy Works
(or Doesn't)

IN THEORY, THE PEOPLE are the bedrock of democracy. They elect TDs to govern in line with the policies and commitments given during the election campaign. The TDs elect a taoiseach, who chooses a Cabinet and a range of junior ministers. The Cabinet collectively decides the legislation and ministerial decisions that will be implemented; the parliament scrutinizes all this and passes it into law.

The government, in theory, acts as a kind of referee – watching events, thinking ahead, hearing the opinions and aspirations of all sides, and deciding fairly on what is the right course to take.

In practice, the great bulk of the TDs have no effective role. They spend most of their time working to be re-elected. They go into the Dáil chamber when necessary, usually to vote. If you've watched Dáil broadcasts on TV you might have seen the practice of doughnutting. TDs move from their seats to bunch up around the speaker. In close shots, the speaker seems to be surrounded by TDs, in a full Dáil. In reality, vast stretches of seats are empty.

The debates are meaningless to most TDs most of the time. They're told, by party whips, how to vote. If they disobey, they are put out of the parliamentary party. An example of how this works was seen in March 2012, when Fine Gael TD Peter Mathews put down a proposal at an Oireachtas Finance Committee meeting. He was then told the party bigshots disagreed with the proposal, and was told to vote against his own motion, and he did so.

That was on an issue of some passing importance. Far more important decisions, some that will ripple down through the future, affecting the lives of our children and their children, are taken with minimal parliamentary oversight.

The system of whips, and the rigid imposition of the will of the party hierarchy, transfers power from the parliament to the political parties.

Every now and then a TD will vote against the party line, usually when faced with a measure that adversely affects local voters. This is in hopes of maintaining his or her seat at the next election. Even this apparent rebellion is often arranged – a little drama acted out for the benefit of the constituency voters. The party prefers to hold on to the seat, even at the cost of allowing a little rebellion – and, for this, the TD must be allowed to be seen as a martyr. The TD is almost always taken back on to the official party ticket before the next general election.

The parliament as a whole is supposed to legislate. It doesn't. The Cabinet is supposed to execute the wishes of parliament. It doesn't.

The Cabinet runs everything, handing down legislation for the TDs to rubber-stamp. Since the taoiseach can reshuffle Cabinet members to the backbenches, the Cabinet is deferential to the wishes of the taoiseach and his sidekicks.

Again, in theory, the Cabinet acts as a neutral, fair, balanced mediator, making decisions without fear or favour. Without going into it in any detail, the evidence is clear that, in modern times, Irish politicians are deeply embedded with powerful, wealthy people. Their deference, even in public, is nauseating. They socialize with wealthy interests, they seek advice from them, they accept money from them in the form of political donations. They are aware of the largesse of these people, and they're aware of these people's power should they be discommoded.

Above all, they identify with these people, seeing them as partners in the management of their little part of the world.

In recent times, even the Cabinet has been sidelined by the creation of the Economic Management Council, of which there are just four members: the Taoiseach, Tánaiste, Minister for Finance and Minister for Public Expenditure and Reform (Cutter-in-Chief). They meet each Wednesday, along with five unelected officials and two unelected political 'advisers', and they take all economic decisions. These decisions set the parameters within which the Cabinet is allowed to make decisions.

There are politicians who get into politics because they feel strongly about something. But a large number of TDs win a seat and spend decades in the Dáil without ever consciously engaging with political issues. It's a job. They look after the constituency and vote as the party whip tells them, for bills they may or may not have read.

They're for jobs and against unemployment.

They're against 'red tape' and for enterprise.

They're for the taxpayer and against 'faceless bureaucrats'.

They're for peace and against violence.

They want lower taxes but they also want a hospital built or retained in their constituency.

The most electorally successful politician of his era, Bertie Ahern, governed throughout the inflating of the Celtic Bubble. On the Northern conflict, he was for peace, so he worked hard to support the process that was under way when he took office. Beyond that, many believe he was for whatever made him and his party more electorally popular.

Economically, Ahern was for stability, managing things so they appeared to be ticking over. He seems to have been unaware of the reality of the economy over which he presided.

The parties are dominated by professional politicians who will take whatever side of an issue will win them more votes. Only a handful of politicians have half a grasp of any ideas – and these can dominate the politics of a government.

Among the ministers in the years leading up to the economic collapse, from 1997 to 2011, only Mary Harney, Michael McDowell and Charlie McCreevy seemed to have a bigger agenda than to hold on to power. And it seemed as though their grasp was that of someone who had come across the politics of free-market extremism and been impressed enough to buy a book on the subject, and even to read some of it.

Media coverage of all this largely revolved around party politics – the share of first preferences, constituency power bases and alliances at national level.

In those vital years when the economy was being steadily undermined, McCreevy and Harney made the running and Fianna Fáil wallowed in the new and brash version of capitalism

Michael McDowell attracted headlines with his attack on the notion of equality. 'A dynamic liberal economy like ours demands flexibility and inequality in some respects to function.' It is such inequality 'which provides incentives'.

At national level, even in dealing with the new economics of the kick-ass markets, Fianna Fáilism brought only the ethics of parish-pump glad-handing and backstabbing.

Fine Gael was much the same, only not so good at the game. We, they said, could do that better.

Labour spoke of principles – and it attracted many who believed in those principles – but, nationally, despite occasional rhetoric and electoral bravado, it never saw its role as anything other than propping up a bigger party.

Sinn Féin was for long seen as Fianna Fáil with guns. Then, they binned the guns and adopted a strategy for taking office.

Towards the end, the Greens joined government, but although they claimed to have a wide range of policies, they had little to say about anything beyond the Green issues.

We desperately need democratic structures that function – that protect citizens from the huge and brutal forces of finance and special interests. We need a democratic shield against the attacks of the golden circles who unashamedly see themselves as predators and the rest of us as prey.

What we have is a parliament of TDs deprived of their powers by the party whip system, and with no apparent wish to exercise the power they have under the constitution. As a parliament, it's a dead duck, dominated by an overweening Cabinet, within which a handful of ministers hold sway.

The political ambitions of the governing parties don't go much beyond a desire to kill off Fianna Fáil. External forces – the ECB, the EU commission, the IMF and the US Treasury – ensure the Cabinet doesn't get any notions of placing the interests of the citizens above those of the bankers.

That Cabinet is surrounded by those huge and brutal forces of finance and special interests. To some of us, it appears to be a plaything of those forces.

22

How Laws are Made (or Not)

THE BUDGET DETAILS WERE contained in the three hundred pages of the 2012 Finance Bill. If you looked at Section 14 thereof you found something called the 'Special Assignee Relief Programme' (SARP).

It sounds like a charitable scheme to protect the poorest among us, those in most need of respite from the afflictions of the world. In fact, it's a charitable scheme that has the effect of boosting the income of some of the best-paid people on the planet.

All of what follows is above board, entirely within the legal and ethical rules of parliament. No strokes were pulled, no one did anything wrong; this is routine.

SARP-type tax breaks were already in existence from 2008, but this was a refining exercise. It was aimed at employees who are brought into this country by foreign companies and paid between €75,000 and €500,000 a year. The thinking behind the SARP tax relief is that it will encourage the appointment of all sorts of geniuses who might otherwise not bestow their talents upon Ireland.

Although a similar scheme was in place for almost four years, there's no evidence that there was any assessment of how many of these geniuses it brought to our shores, or what benefit we derived from their coming. Companies do not employ people to create benefits for the wider community. Unsurprisingly, they pay them to benefit the company.

SARP 2012 made 30 per cent of the salary of such Top People exempt from tax for up to five years. And the state would subsidize the cost of these geniuses sending their children to private, fee-paying schools, at up to €5,000 tax relief per year. Thoughtfully, the act also gave a tax break for an annual return trip to wherever the executive came from, along with his or her spouse or civil partner and a child.

The bill became an act and, some months later, Carl O'Brien of the *Irish Times* acquired, through the Freedom of Information legislation, some documents relating to the creation of this scheme. He used them to explore how lobbying works when laws are being written.

These documents showed that between March and September of 2011, the Department of Finance received a number of submissions from outfits representing multinationals. They included the usual accountancy and banking groups: KPMG, Deloitte and Citibank, the employers' lobby group IBEC, and something called the IFSC Clearing House Group.

The Clearing House Group, according to Taoiseach Enda Kenny, is 'a forum for the exchange of views and the co-ordination of effort'. The clout this group has is shown by the fact that it's chaired by the Secretary General of the Taoiseach's Department.

In the run-up to the 2012 Budget, the Clearing House Group arranged meetings between senior government representatives and a range of finance outfits, from JP Morgan to Ernst & Young, from Barclays to HSBC, not to mention zombies such as the Bank of Ireland and AIB.

Out of some Clearing House Group discussions, the *Irish Times* documents showed, tax consultants Deloitte were given the job of proposing specific demands for inclusion in the Budget, in relation to SARP. It is reported that Deloitte sent this material to the Department of Finance in September 2011.

Within a month, civil servants had outlined the main points in a memo for Michael Noonan. The memo sought approval for the scheme, but a handwritten note pointed out that there might be a bit of negative comment 'on grounds of equity'. After all, the Budget would also be cutting services and creating further charges for everyone else to pay.

Seven weeks later, Noonan announced that the SARP scheme would be in his Budget. He gave no details.

The details were leaked to the *Irish Times* on 8 February 2012. The next day, after some discussion, a chap from a leading accountancy firm was given the job of emailing a Finance civil servant, offering a meeting with 'senior people in the industry' and declaring that he 'would be glad to be part of the discussion if you thought that would be helpful'.

A week later, presumably after taking advice from the 'senior people in the industry', civil servants sent a memo to Noonan, looking for changes. Noonan said yes. Six weeks later the tax break was law.

Some finance people believed it wasn't sufficiently generous. And, although the whole point of the exercise was to attract geniuses who would generate wealth, Shaun Murphy, Head of Tax and Legal Services at KPMG, later wrote that it was 'unlikely to attract key talent'.

No net increase in 'key talent', no assessment of whether there was anything in this to be gained by the citizens, but a tax break designed for a specific category of people.

That's an example of how a law can come into being with the

cooperation of the finance business. In *The Corporate Takeover of Ireland*, Kieran Allen gave a couple of examples of laws that never made it on to the statute book.

The Alcohol Product Bill was drawn up in 2005. Then, as before and since, there was a lot of concern about the consequences of the abuse of alcohol – bad health, violence and death – particularly among the young. The bill was a small, measured attempt to do something useful: it would regulate the advertising of alcohol aimed at young people – the kind of adverts that suggested that getting pissed would win you crowds of friends, and puking your guts up in an alley would do wonders for your sex life.

Regulating such advertising could be a useful part of a campaign to reduce health-wrecking alcohol binges. The move had the backing of health professionals.

Using PR outfits and intense lobbying, the drinks business waged a systematic campaign. The law was dropped.

Doing nothing wouldn't look good, so the politicians cobbled together a 'voluntary code', weak and pointless. No regulation, just a promise of good behaviour.

Michael McLoughlin, a director of central services with the National Youth Federation, was quoted in the *Irish Independent*: 'It appears that the drinks industry is now in control of the agenda. Every time young people gather we are treated to lectures from politicians about drinking and bad behaviour – yet this is the government's response.'

Two years earlier, at a time when it might have made a real difference, and prevented the worst of the economic collapse that followed, there was an attempt to impose a feeble measure of regulation on the finance business. The reputation of Dublin as a financial Wild West was what made the more sober business people somewhat uneasy. Government intervention was required.

The Companies (Audit and Accounting) Bill 2003 was to apply

only to companies with a turnover greater than €15.3 million. The bill required company directors to declare that they were satisfied there were sufficient controls in place to ensure compliance with the law. Not exactly draconian. This required directors to sign a form that indicated they'd put in place the standard protections to ensure the company didn't break the law. And the auditors would have to declare they had checked this was true.

The usual suspects came forth to declare that this was a disincentive that would sap the abilities of the wealth creators. Big accountancy firms let it be known they weren't happy, and the usual friends of business made tut-tut noises. The government folded. The law was stopped, passed to a review group for adjusting – the review group included bankers and people who work with and for bankers. The regulatory effort – already weak – was watered down to pointlessness.

Among the voices that howled down the measure was that of what the *Irish Times* described as 'a leading banker', who warned that the legislation would 'drive up costs, discourage investment and damage competitiveness'. Yes, it was wee Seanie FitzPatrick, Anglo Irish Bank chief executive, addressing the Institute of Directors. The bill, he said, would stifle business with over-regulation.

Sometimes, major developments pass through the Oireachtas hardly noticed by TDs. Under the Fianna Fáil/PD regime, there was a gold rush to build private hospitals, and widen the two-tier gap in the health service, facilitated by tax breaks. These were included in late amendments to finance bills in 2001 and 2003, to which the vast majority of politicians paid no attention.

In theory, the government creates laws for the common good, and we all have an equal say in urging what laws should be passed. In practice, there are strong, tough forces at work, using professional lobbying firms, with contacts in all the places that matter, pushing continuously to pressure politicians. This can create a law, or nobble another law. It can push government in directions that help the business interests of those forces.

These forces concern themselves not alone with law but with policy. And, just as the policies that resulted in the economic crash were influenced by these forces, we can be sure that not a day goes by that those forces aren't hard at work influencing the current austerity policies.

23

How the Elites Explain Themselves (or Don't)

THE ELITES WITHIN IRELAND and within the EU and elsewhere have made huge decisions that affect us and will affect the next generation, controversial decisions that create mass unemployment and will do so for years.

In theory, such decisions are made within a democratic framework – an essential part of which involves the decision makers explaining what they are doing and why. That's why the media is more than just a set of competing commercial enterprises. The elites explain themselves to the media, and the media conveys this information to the citizens.

Often, such matters are conveyed in vague reports, heavy with jargon and usually wrapped in vague terms of 'jobs', 'recovery' or 'commitments given by the previous government'. There's information in there, but it's expressed in a lazy, obscure way.

Often, Official Ireland will deliberately misinform, using statements that conceal more than they reveal. And some sections of the media will just pass it on, unworried about being complicit in the lies. There are also cheerleaders for the elites, who propagandize on their behalf. At its best, the media will assess the stories the people they admire want passed on and measure them against known facts, asking questions and demanding more detail.

Below, here are two occasions on which a journalist sought information on an important issue, the decision that the Irish state would pay unguaranteed bondholders every cent it didn't owe them. The bondholders gambled and lost, but Irish politicians decided to pay them as though they had won. Billion after billion after billion.

The 'unguaranteed' bit is important. One could argue against paying any bank bondholders, in any circumstances, since they bet on a bank that failed – but this concerns a starker issue. The politicians have persisted in paying billions of euro to bondholders to whom no guarantee applies, where there is no political, legal or moral reason to pay.

It's even worse. By 2011, we had paid off a lot of the Irish bankers' debts to European bankers. Let Michael Noonan explain, in the Dáil, before becoming Minister for Finance:

> The latest available bank data shows that Irish guaranteed bank debt has been sold on at a discount to hedge funds in the USA, the UK and Luxembourg, as well as to smaller speculative investors . . . They are no longer being held by European banks that lent the money in the first instance. Rather, they are now in the possession of hedge funds.
>
> *Deputy Pat Rabbitte*: They will make a killing on it . . .
>
> *Deputy Michael Noonan*: The position has now become indefensible, that the Irish taxpayer, even the poorest taxpayers, should be required to underpin the speculation of hedge-fund investors.

To treat such bank debt as 'our debt', with politicians saying 'We'll never default', is just madness. But they did it, blustering on.

In this chapter, we use the experiences of Vincent Browne of TV3 asking questions about this matter. There are other important issues, and there are other persevering interviewers who are denied answers, but these are clear examples of the arrogant belief that neither the political class nor the Troika technicians need explain themselves.

In the first of these instances, on *Tonight with Vincent Browne*, a Labour politician was asked about the decision to pay unguaranteed bondholders. The politician was Dominic Hannigan, a new TD. Hannigan isn't one of the Dáil's muppets, he's obviously intelligent and energetic, highly educated, with a Master's degree in finance. As a public representative, and a member of one of the governing parties, Hannigan is obliged to explain himself.

An appearance in the media isn't a publicity event, to boost a politician's profile. In modern life, it's part of the means by which politicians supposedly engage with the citizenry, explaining and arguing their policies. Without such engagement, and the debate that should follow, a vote every four or five years is meaningless.

Here's how an intelligent and energetic politician, in April 2012, evades answering a question on an extremely important issue. And, in so doing, exposes the manner in which the elites refuse to engage with the democratic process on the policies that affect the citizens.

Browne: *We paid another 1.5 billion two weeks ago to unsecured bond-holders. It's just incredible. And there was no acknowledgement, no debate about it, no fuss about it, no nothing. Can you understand, Dominic, why we continue to do this?*

Hannigan: *Well, yes, because we're in a situation that we want to get out of as soon as possible. Don't forget the country was virtually bankrupt, Vincent, when we took over—*

Browne: *Why are we paying 1.5 billion to unsecured bondholders?*

Hannigan: *The important thing that this country has to do is regain its reputation on the international stage to reap some of the benefits—*

Browne: *Why did we pay 1.5 billion to unguaranteed bondholders in AIB?*

Hannigan: *Because, as I said, we're trying to make sure that we regain our reputation abroad. Just this week we've seen some of the benefits of regaining that reputation. We've seen international investments. Today, just before we came on air, we saw the taoiseach and the tánaiste in Dun Laoghaire announcing more jobs for the country. We want to see more of that, but we can only get more foreign investment by regaining the confidence of international investors. And that's what we're trying to do, slowly, slowly, but surely.*

Browne: *Grand. Do you think the confidence of investors is improved by our recklessness in paying a debt we don't own?*

Hannigan: *Well, I think the recklessness came a long time ago—*

Browne: *Don't mind that, don't tell us about that. Just deal with the question. We're paying 1.5 billion for debt we don't own. And we've no legal obligation to pay, no moral obligation. It's not part of any deal we did with the Troika, nothing. We're paying this 1.5 billion, we did it two weeks ago – why? What's the justification for that?*

Hannigan: *I only wish when we came into government that we had a clean book—*

Browne: *Just, please don't make speeches about tangential issues when I'm asking a question. What is the reason that we paid €1.5 billion to unguaranteed bondholders in AIB two weeks ago?*

Hannigan: *Because as a nation we need to stay above the line, we need to make sure that we pay our debts—*

Browne: *And how does that— '. . . pay our debts'? That's not our debt.*

Hannigan: *So that we can—*

Browne: *It is not our debt, Dominic.*

Hannigan: *And we're going to be borrowing for the next few years . . .*

Browne: *Dominic, it is not our debt.*

Hannigan: *Well, you know, Vincent, you have to look at it like this – the government made commitments, the last government made commitments in relation to bank bail-outs that we as a sovereign government now have to live up to . . .*

Browne: *This has nothing got to do—*

Hannigan: *We have to pay back—*

Browne: *Do you understand? This has nothing to do with the bank guarantee. Not covered by the bank guarantee. We have no legal obligation, no moral obligation, no obligation at all to pay this debt – why did we do it?*

Hannigan: *It's an easy solution for you to sit here and say, 'Oh, let's not pay this debt' – but the reality is—*

Browne: *But why don't you tell us why we do it?*

Hannigan: *As a government we have to make sure that we have access to funding so that we can pay for those services out there, like our nurses, like our social security; we need to make sure that that money is in the bank—*

Browne: *It's just incredible, you won't – you – you – I've never come across this before, even in talking to politicians, that somebody just waffles on and on. Completely ignoring the question—*

Hannigan: *Ah, I'm sure you have, Vincent—*

Browne: *—completely ignoring the question, so we'll try again now. We paid €1.5 billion to AIB bondholders, debt we had no responsibility for. Neither the people of the country, nor the state had no responsibility for. Nor did the state have any legal obligation to do this. No moral obligation, no obligation under the deal we have with the Troika, or anything else. Why did we do that?*

Hannigan: *I think you need to look at the benefits of making sure that we pay back loans and debts such as this—*

Browne: *It's not ours! What's the benefit of paying back—*

Hannigan: *One thing that we've managed to do since we came in just fifteen months ago, what we've managed to do is we've managed to cut 10 billion off our interest—*

Browne: *What's this got to do with the question? What's it got to do – please, Dominic, I just give up, you win, you win—*

Hannigan: *Vincent, Vincent—*

Browne: *You win, I just give up, I give up, I give up, I give up.*

As Vincent said at the time, Mr Hannigan demonstrated great skill in evading the issue. Here, he used his undoubted talents to deprive any viewers, any voters, of even minimal information about his stance on a crucial issue. Asked why unguaranteed bondholders should be paid, he spoke about Enda Kenny and Eamon Gilmore announcing new jobs that day. Challenged on why he used the term 'our debts' for debts that clearly are not ours, he spoke of nurses and social security. Mr Hannigan is not unique. This is a standard technique among politicians, and it reduces debate to an exchange of meaningless verbiage.

The second example is from January 2012. Envoys from the Troika, which sets the parameters for the Economic Management Council, made one of their periodic visits. Here are technocrats with no connection to the country, with no electoral mandate, making decisions that have serious effects on the citizens. To retain any credibility whatever, the very least they could do was explain in some detail what they were doing, and why – and answer any questions that might be put to them. In a gesture to accountability, it was their habit to hold a press conference before leaving the country.

On this occasion, one of these people, Klaus Masuch, a senior executive with the European Central Bank, somewhat patronizingly referred to his experiences with Dublin taxi drivers and how 'they are often very, very informed, I must say, very, very informed'.

Subsequently, Vincent Browne put the following question.

Browne: *Klaus Masuch, did your taxi driver tell you how the Irish people are bewildered that we are required to pay unguaranteed bondholders billions of euros for debts that the Irish people have no relation to or no bearing with, primarily to bail out or to ensure the solvency of European banks? And if the taxi driver had asked you that question, what would have been your response? That's my first question.*

(At that stage, Barbara Nolan, head of the European Commission representation in Ireland, sitting beside Mr Masuch, intervened.)

Nolan: *Well – well – well – can we take a couple together? Can you ask the second question?*

Browne: *Well, my second question is a completely different issue and it may have a follow-through if Mr Masuch doesn't answer the question in a way that would illuminate the taxi driver's understanding of all this. I would have a follow-through question.*

Nolan: *Right, can I ask you then to pass the mic, and we'll come back to you for the second question?*

Browne: *Well, if you don't mind, that's a way of breaking up the exchange, and I would prefer if it went this way: We've a tradition in Irish journalism that we pursue issues and that when somebody doesn't ask [answer] a question we follow through on it, and I hope that tradition will be respected on this occasion. So could you answer the question?*

Masuch: *I have answered a very similar question of you – I think it was two reviews ago – and can . . . and I answered it. I can understand that this is a difficult decision to be made by the government and there's no doubt about it but there are different aspects of the problem to be, to be balanced against each other. And I can understand that the government came to, came to the view that, all in all, the costs for the, for Irish people, for the, for the stability of the banking system, for the confidence in the banking system of taking a certain action in this respect, which you are mentioning, could likely have been much bigger than the benefits for the taxpayer which of course would have been there. So the financial sector would have been affected, the confidence of the financial sector would have been negatively affected, and I can understand that there were, that there was a difficult decision but that the decision was taken in this direction.*

Browne: *That, that – well, that doesn't address the issue. We are required to pay, in respect of a defunct bank – that has no bearing on the welfare of the Irish people at all – we are required to pay in respect of this defunct bank, billions on unguaranteed bonds in order to ensure the health of European banks. Now how would you explain that situation to the taxi driver that you talked about earlier?*

Masuch: *I think I have addressed the question.*

Browne: *No, you haven't addressed the question because you referred to the viability of the Irish financial institutions. This financial institution I'm talking about is defunct. It's over. It's finished. Now, why are the Irish people required, under threat from the ECB, why are the Irish people required to pay billions to unguaranteed bond-holders under threat from the ECB?*

[Masuch didn't answer.]

Browne: *You didn't answer the question the last time so maybe you'll answer it this time.*

Nolan: *Well, I think he doesn't have anything to add to what he's already said. Can I . . .*

Browne: *Well, just a minute now. This isn't, this isn't good enough. You people are intervening in this society, causing huge damage by requiring us to make payments not for the benefit of anybody in Ireland but for the benefit of European financial institutions.*

Now, could you explain why the Irish people are inflicted with this burden?

Masuch: *Well, I think I have addressed the question.*

Browne: *You've nothing to say. There's no answer, is that right? Is that it? No answer?*

Masuch: *I have given an answer.*

Browne: *You have given an answer that didn't address the question.*

Nolan: *That's your view.*

Browne: *That is my view and I think it would be the view of the taxi driver and a few of our viewers tonight.*

Nolan: *Right. Can we please move on?*

After that, it became the habit of such senior EU personnel to leave for the airport at the end of their visits, without bothering to make themselves available for media questioning. This left no engagement between the EU personnel and the Irish media or citizens.

No doubt they imparted all relevant information to their taxi drivers.

24

Ask the Experts

MANY YEARS BACK, THE old *Evening Press* had a regular and very popular feature called 'Ask the Experts'. Whatever your problem or query, you wrote to the newspaper and they'd get an expert on the job. Probably the feature was written by some underpaid journalist who phoned a mechanic, a lawyer, a medic, a linguist, or whoever might be able to pass on the advice being sought. But the impression given was that the *Evening Press* kept a battalion of 'Experts' from a range of specialities in a back room on Burgh Quay, instantly ready to provide the correct answer to anything that might bother the readers.

In those innocent days there was a great belief in Experts. It was understood that there were right ways and wrong ways to do things. And that there were Experts who could infallibly pronounce on which was which. Experts were seen as people so thoroughly schooled in their disciplines that their answers would be drawn from a deep well of knowledge, thoroughly tested and beyond challenge.

These days, we're less trusting. We know there are a variety of opinions on most issues, and the views of experts, while better informed, are not always conclusive. As often as not, an expert is in the pay of one side or another in any dispute. Experts are often too close to their subject, too trusting of their sources, unwilling to challenge the consensus. It's always safer for an expert to give an authoritative opinion on the style and cut of the emperor's new clothes than to suggest that the emperor is in the nip.

Here, for instance, is an expert opinion.

It was produced in 2007 by a New York management consultancy called Oliver Wyman. This company came together from a number of other highly regarded firms, pooling their talents, making OW an ace among aces. These experts didn't just think for a day or two and issue an opinion, they assembled masses of information then used their proprietary assessment tool, their Shareholder Performance Index, to analyse it. Like all the best people, Oliver Wyman doesn't come cheap. But, hey, that's the free market. You get what you pay for.

Let's say it's 2007 and you're looking for somewhere to invest your hard-earned money, with a view to getting the best return. And you had access to Oliver Wyman's exclusive, proprietary Shareholder Performance Index, not available from any lesser firms of financial experts. Here's what you'd find. You'd find that Oliver Wyman had measured 170 of the world's top companies against its SPI and the firm's experts had ranked each one on its average market value over the past year. And Oliver Wyman had produced a list showing the top twenty investment targets.

Let's give you just the top five. And in true beauty-contest format, let's give them in reverse order.

At number 5: China Life Assurance Company.

At number 4: QBE Insurance Group, Australia.

Coming up fast at number 3: Sberbank, Russia.

Almost made it to the top, at number 2: Chicago Mercantile Exchange.

And, at number 1 of 170, the best of the best . . . Anglo Irish Bank.

The year after this list was drawn up, Anglo's bubble burst.

This wasn't just a hiccup for Oliver Wyman. The previous year, their expertise had produced a report that named Anglo Irish as one of four examples of 'supermodel' banks 'that provide better and more focused propositions . . . Players who have adopted these models have grown at twice the pace of the market as a whole.'

Of course, we could fill another book with quotes from cheerleaders of the Celtic Tiger who urged people to buy, buy, buy. Hardly a newspaper pundit or radio disc jockey let a week go by without telling people they were fools not to borrow money and buy property, because prices would endlessly go in one direction – up, up, up.

But such recklessness was a product of the bubble, not its cause. Anyone who gambled on the say-so of a newspaper or radio commentator was being foolish. Most people, though, listened carefully to the experts. Here's a small, representative sample:

Auctioneer Ken McDonald: 'As one who has been involved in the Irish property market for forty years . . . I am totally convinced that the market is currently in good shape and that anyone buying now will do extremely well in the years ahead. There is no better investment than Irish property at present' (*Sunday Independent*, 25 March 2007).

And, having moved from the ECB to become economics editor of the *Irish Times*, then to become economics editor of *Newstalk FM*, Marc Coleman was of the opinion that: 'Far from an economic storm – or a property shock – Ireland's economy is set to rock and roll into the century' (*Sunday Independent*, 23 September 2007).

In the Seanad, on 10 April 2008, Fianna Fáil veteran Donie Cassidy had advice for young people: 'Now is the right time to buy. We have a duty to tell first-time house buyers, young couples

ASK THE EXPERTS   177

with no previous experience, that there is unbelievable value in the marketplace today. It will not last for ever. It is never the wrong time to do the right thing.' He predicted prices would rise by up to 30 per cent over the next eighteen months. Senator Cassidy's expertise derived from his own extensive property investments.

So, we had Oliver Wyman, a leading management consultancy, internationally lauded.

A leading Irish property auctioneer, Ken McDonald.

A leading broadcaster, Marc Coleman, who worked for the Department of Finance and the ECB before becoming economics editor of the *Irish Times*.

Donie Cassidy, property investor and Leader of the House in the Seanad.

A fair cross section of the experts who didn't see it coming, each of them representative of battalions of similar experts in their fields. And, for those special occasions when nerves needed calming, the media had in reserve extra-special experts.

There is no more respected expert than Peter Sutherland. When called on to bestow his expertise upon us, Peter is often described as the 'former Attorney General'. In fact, that was a small part of Peter's life. He was appointed AG by his close friend Garret FitzGerald for one period of nine months and another of two years. That was twenty-eight years ago.

Peter went into the corporate world, where he became a major player. He was a director of the Royal Bank of Scotland, but he's best known as chairman of Goldman Sachs International. Peter is a banker, respected on several continents. His economic expertise was highly regarded by the kind of people who are impressed by that sort of thing – so they made him chair of the London School of Economics.

In March 2008, behind the cheerful image of Official Ireland, there was unease. A Merrill Lynch analyst named Philip Ingram wrote a controversial report that questioned the solidity of the Irish banks, finding them deeply in hock to commercial property deals. Irish bankers were furious and Merrill Lynch withdrew the report.

Two months later, bank shares were beginning to slide.

In April 2008, Peter Sutherland gave a speech to the Irish Management Institute, urging optimism on those uneasy about the construction industry, and the implications for the banking system. As the expert's expert, Peter's remarks were widely reported. The RTÉ news website: 'He said a building slowdown did not represent the same systemic risk to the Irish economy that would have been the case in the US.'

The 'building slowdown' was turning into the collapse of the construction business – and, with that, the collapse of government revenue and catastrophe for the banks. Foolishly, the government had followed its tax-cutting agenda by becoming unsustainably dependent on stamp duty. As the building industry came to a halt, it lost those taxes, and the income tax from the wages of building workers.

Peter seemed unaware that there was indeed a 'systemic risk' in the building slowdown. The banks were already crumbling. Within six months they would be zombie banks, propped up only by the notorious state guarantee. Behind the scenes, the government and the civil servants were already frantically trying to find a magic bullet to slay the monster they saw rising from the mess they had made.

The *Irish Examiner* reported the same IMI speech, telling us that Peter said Ireland should beware of 'talking itself into a crisis'. It was a common phrase within Official Ireland – as though the crisis wasn't actually happening; it was all in our heads.

'The fact is that the achievements made in the Irish economy are real,' Peter said. 'They are not a bubble and, given the proper policies, the Irish economy can confidently look forward to continuing growth above the EU average for the next five years and beyond.'

This was so far from what was about to happen that it needs no comment.

Exactly a year later, in April 2009, Peter was writing in the *Financial Times*. Under the headline: 'Celtic Tiger Sharpens its Claws for Recovery', he wrote about 'the underlying health of the Irish economy'. Most of us saw an economy that was nose-diving, unemployment spiralling. Peter saw the silver lining. 'Once Ireland overcomes this short-term panic . . . the basic strengths of the Irish economy remain formidable.'

Like most such respected experts, Peter saw austerity as the answer. He approved the 'harsh measures necessary'.

Three years later, an economy deflated by harsh measures is in dire trouble. Experts were all over the place, telling us to forget the past, don't play the blame game, we are where we are, and we're turning the corner.

How could so many experts, including someone so respected in Official Ireland as Peter Sutherland, be so wrong about the depth of the crisis?

Because the bankers, the politicians, the economists, had for decades been given a free rein. They had fashioned the world in their own image. How, at this stage, could they be expected to do anything else but believe totally in their own view of the world, which said that, as long as they maintained confidence in the markets, all would be well?

The lucky punters at that IMI conference also had the benefit of the wisdom of Bertie Ahern, who assured them that the Irish banking system remained sound and robust. He knew, as only a taoiseach who had been in office for eleven years could know, that 'capital adequacy ratios and the quality of loan books, as well as the ability of the banks to fund their operations, all continue to signal a strong state of health for the industry here.'

But wait – weren't there independent think-tank economists who—

The Economic and Social Research Institute (ESRI)? Yes, and they're smart people. In its 2005 midterm report, the ESRI warned: 'There are considerable dangers in the current situation: in particular the very high level of dependence on the building industry.'

And the ESRI was, in effect, told to bugger off.

Perhaps chastened by the warnings against talking down the economy, the ESRI, in its midterm review of May 2008, was quite cheerful: 'The Irish economy is resilient.' GNP growth would continue at almost 4 per cent a year, and 'the fundamentals of the Irish economy are sound'.

At that stage, the Department of Finance was tearing its hair out as it dawned that the banks were about to go down the toilet. Within four months the floor would open up under the economy.

And when the economy crashed, what happened to the experts?

Remember Oliver Wyman, the New York consultants who in 2007 produced a list that had Anglo Irish as a prime investment? In 2009, they were hired to help Bank of Ireland. In 2010, they were on the payroll at Irish Life and Permanent. In 2012, they were hired by the Spanish government to assess Spain's banks. The same year, they were hired to audit Permanent TSB. And the Financial Regulator has them on a panel of experts, to be called on when needed.

Experts who prove less than astute in their understanding of what is happening, and what should be done – whether they be economists, bankers or high-price consultants – shrug off their failures and move on. The media and the rest of Official Ireland are lost without supposed experts – to quote and to trust. They need to believe that someone knows what's happening.

So, when the economy crashed, the elites turned again to their experts and said, *What do we do now?*

You must re-establish confidence in the markets.

How?

You pile on the austerity. You show that the citizens are willing to tighten their belts and pay for the crisis. You show that the state will cover the failed gambles of the bankers.

And it didn't matter that year after year of austerity resulted in an economy spiralling downward. Austerity was their message, it would always be their message, for that's what it said in their theories. The same theories that made some people very, very rich – and then blew up one economy after another.

On 22 September 2011, as the government prepared another austerity budget, RTÉ's *Morning Ireland* called on Peter Sutherland to give the nation a taste of his wisdom. In the introduction, listeners were told that Peter's 'is not a voice that can be easily ignored'.

That was true only to the extent that the media so relentlessly pumped his voice into our heads.

Peter told *Morning Ireland* listeners that austerity should be 'front-loaded'. More of it, and faster. And it was working. 'We've begun to turn a corner,' he said, using the hackneyed phrase that had been thrown at us from the beginning of the crisis to justify every failed twist and turn of Official Ireland's disastrous policies.

His message was no different from what a backbench government TD, or indeed a county councillor, might have said. Bog-standard austerity. What mattered was that Peter was a man of substance, a former Attorney General, a big wheel at Goldman Sachs. An expert.

But Peter was something else. He was a very comfortable man. Like so many who preached austerity, he was proposing pain for other people, pain he was unlikely ever to feel.

Peter had a long life in the corporate world, at the highest levels, and was rewarded accordingly. The *Sunday Independent* Rich List claimed Peter had amassed a fortune of €80 million. He had an income from his position with the famously generous Goldman Sachs. He was at that time also chair of BP, the oil company.

For his contribution to public life, his two years and nine months as Attorney General twenty-eight years ago, he was drawing a pension of €50,000 a year from the Irish state. Peter was one of many people who received an extraordinary pension for a short period of work done for the state decades ago, and for which he was appropriately rewarded at the time.

It's hard to see how anyone so well-heeled could ever suffer, whatever the austerity measures imposed. And it would take an immense act of imagination for someone in that position to see beyond the tired old tools of austerity and creating 'confidence'.

Not all experts have Peter's cushion of money to protect them from the austerity which they propagandize. But most are in the upper regions of the income tables.

No doubt they genuinely believe that harsh measures applied to the low- and medium-paid might be the best way to solve the crisis. And they equally genuinely believe that radical measures that would inflict real losses on those at the top of the wealth table would not work.

But then, they would, wouldn't they?

25

We're Not Listening,
We're Not Listening

IT IS RARE FOR a Dáil deputy to bluntly tackle one of the great scandals of our times: the transfer of debt from private gamblers to citizens. One man did so in words that stung. This is from the Dáil record of 15 December 2010:

> What legal or moral compulsion is on Ireland, however,
> to honour in full debt incurred by Irish banks when there
> was no state involvement in the arrangements? These
> loans were entered into freely by willing lenders and bor-
> rowers, with absolutely no state participation. The interest
> rate charged represented the risk at the time, and there
> never was a state liability. It is obscene that liability for
> these loans is now being transferred to the Irish taxpayer,
> in many respects to the poorest of the Irish taxpayers.
>
> The Irish government and the taxpayer has no liability
> whatsoever for these debts . . . In the Budget, the

> Minister for Finance reduced social welfare payments,
> punished the blind, disabled, widows, carers and the
> unemployed and he taxed the poorest at work, and for
> what? It was so that the taxpayer can take on liability
> for debts the country never incurred, and arose from
> private arrangements between private institutions. What a
> disaster and an obscenity.

The Dáil deputy was, of course, Fine Gael's Michael Noonan. He was attacking Fianna Fáil's Minister for Finance, Brian Lenihan. Less than three months later, following a general election, Mr Noonan was appointed Minister for Finance. Since then, it can be argued that the Fine Gael/Labour government has pursued an obscene course of punishing the blind, disabled, widows, carers and the unemployed, and taxing the poorest at work.

Lenihan professed to believe in the moral integrity of what he was doing. Michael Noonan cannot make that claim. He said himself there is no legal or moral compulsion behind his actions, and he knows that vulnerable people, and the poorest amongst us, are suffering as a result.

Promises were made, the promises won votes, the promises were broken.

Nothing new in that, but after the 2011 election the blatant way the promises were shrugged off was more shameless than usual. With a huge parliamentary majority, Cabinet ministers effectively asked, 'What ya gonna do about it?'

The democratic model is broken. There is no longer any connection whatever between the voters and the parties and what happens in government.

Few could disagree that the transfer of immense private debts on to the backs of citizens is morally wrong. But some argue that we have to leave morality out of it. They say we can live with an immoral policy if it produces results. So, how's that going? Is it producing results?

Almost €70 billion squandered on dead banks, plus whatever NAMA costs. Supporting the banks and screwing the citizens, pleasing the ECB and punishing the blind, disabled, widows, carers and the unemployed has been a disaster. One austerity budget after another, over €20 billion in 'fiscal adjustments', judged by one economist to be 'the largest budgetary adjustments seen anywhere in the advanced economic world in modern times'.

This has suppressed aggregate demand, increasing job losses, leaving businesses to flounder.

In 2010, the Austerity Hawks said their policies would bring unemployment down to 12 per cent by 2012. Back then unemployment was at 14.1 per cent. Far from coming down to 12 per cent by 2012, it went up to 14.8 per cent.

But, hey, we can re-enter the bond markets!

And wave goodbye to the IMF!

The state had to leave the bond markets when interest rates went crazy in the autumn of 2010 – and interest rates went crazy when the bond markets realized how big the bank losses were and how stupid the government had been, taking on bank debt that threatened to sink the state.

And interest rates came down in the summer of 2012, after the ECB signalled its willingness to back some unspecified deal to reduce the bank debt.

But we did get a cut in the interest rate that we pay the Troika for loans!

Government cheerleaders continue to claim that. They lie. The Greeks got a second bail-out, they played hardball, they got an interest-rate reduction. And the Troika had to give Ireland the same reduction.

With debt-to-GDP ratio heading towards an unsustainable

120 per cent by 2014, the Minister for Finance mooches around Europe, pleading for a deal on debt, hoping the Spanish can kick ass and we can ride on their coat-tails – as we did before with the Greeks.

But hey, at least we're all pulling on the green jersey, we're all sharing the pain equally.

Over the period 2008–9, there was a substantial drop in profits.

In 2010, profits bounced back up by 4.4 per cent.

In 2011, profits were up another 6.6 per cent.

And how did workers do?

In 2009, workers' remuneration was down 9.3 per cent.

In 2010, it was down another 6.5 per cent.

And, in 2011, down another 1.4 per cent.

Profits up, wages down: it's policy, not just something that happened. Economist Michael Burke notes what's supposed to happen when there's a transfer of wealth from labour to capital – capital is, in theory, supposed to invest its profits and drive a recovery. Gross Fixed Capital Formation (GFCF) is supposed to go up. 'From 2009 onwards, when profits rose by €8.6 billion, GFCF fell by €9.5 billion.'

The policy, Burke says, of transferring incomes from labour and the poor to capital and the rich, 'which is the real content of austerity, has been an utter failure in reviving growth'.

In 2012, there was supposed to be a rise of 3.25 per cent in economic growth. Instead, there was negligible growth of 0.7 per cent.

Growth comes from market demand, which comes from the mass of the people spending disposable income – which they don't do when they're hit by austerity measures that asset-strip their lives.

So, we can conclude, the policy that involves forcing bankers' debts on to us is not just immoral – it hasn't worked. And the austerity regime of driving down wages to encourage capital to invest – it hasn't worked.

We've got a problem within a problem.

The people in charge know what they're doing is wrong, and they know it doesn't work. However, neither they nor their boosters are open for argument. Their theology says this is what you do, and this is what they'll do, whatever the outcome. It's an article of faith. They believe in austerity like the rest of us believe in gravity.

Doesn't matter what anyone has to say.

An example. In September 2011, the United Nations Conference on Trade and Development (UNCTAD) issued a 190-page report entitled 'Post-crisis Policy Challenges in the World Economy'. It argued that the pursuit of austerity measures and deficit cuts is pushing the world economy towards disaster in a misguided attempt to please global financial markets.

The Secretary General of UNCTAD, Supachai Panitchpakdi, a former head of the World Trade Organisation, said: 'The message here is very pragmatic: we need to reverse our course quickly.' Austerity policies, he said, were 'misconceived and inept' and would lead to a decade of stagnation.

The lead author of the report, Heiner Flassbeck, said: 'If governments stick to the policy of not only keeping fiscal deficits where they are but retrenching, cutting public expenditure, then we will end up in permanent recession.'

The UNCTAD report said, 'A national economy does not function in the same way as an individual firm or household. The latter may be able to increase savings by cutting back spending because such a cutback does not affect its revenues.' However, state cutbacks have a 'negative impact on aggregate demand and the tax base, will lead to lower fiscal revenues and therefore hamper fiscal consolidation'.

And that would lead to? 'An improvement in the immediate cash flow of the government, but with negative consequences for long-term fiscal and debt sustainability.'

What did UNCTAD recommend? 'Wage increases, stricter regulation of financial markets . . . and a conscious break with market-led thinking.'

This report received widespread coverage in the *Daily Telegraph*, the *Guardian*, *The New York Times*, the *Sydney Morning Herald*, and so on. But not in Ireland.

It wasn't that the media were suppressing the report, it's that minds are closed. Group think. Like a kid in an argument, head shaking, hands over ears: *I'm not listening, I'm not listening . . .*

They are locked into their echo chamber, where the only people they speak seriously to – in Ireland, in Europe, in that nice Mr Geithner's office – are fellow Austerity Hawks. They don't reject or suppress contrary arguments, they just don't hear them.

The Austerity Hawks know that such reports don't matter. They are serious people, despite their appalling record. And anything that questions their theology need not even be considered – it's 'for the birds'. The Big Lie in action.

That same month, Enda Kenny's government paid a total of €4.3 billion to gamblers who bet on the Irish banks during the property bubble. The money was paid, as on all such occasions, at the insistence of the Troika.

26

Well, What Would *You* Cut?

I T'S CUSTOMARY FOR BOOKS of this kind to finish with the author's preferred road map to a better world. Others have given their views of how things can be improved: Fintan O'Toole in *Enough is Enough*, Peadar Kirby and Mary Murphy in *Towards a Second Republic*, Kieran Allen in *Ireland's Economic Crash*, as well as the authors of countless articles and blog posts. It's all designed to get a discussion going. Optimistic outfits such as We the Citizens pop up from time to time to suggest that we all get together and work out a sensible and fair way of doing things.

All well-intentioned; all useful up to a point. We could draw from these suggestions a range of ideas for making this a more democratic, fairer, more efficient and more stable society. We could shape it into a manifesto and ask the people to endorse it.

But that's not how things work. When large forces collide, there is no chance of policy papers being exchanged, no debate. The future isn't up for negotiation.

It is the push and pull of various forces within a society that advances things. One set of ideas triumphs, in part or in whole, while another weakens. One section of society benefits, while others lose. Alliances form and compromises are made; pockets of resistance that link up can compel larger forces to make concessions.

The shape of a society that emerges from such tussles can't be laid out in a blueprint. Nor can there be a twelve-step programme towards real change. Ultimately, the deciding element is whether there is a large enough resistance to the failed policies. And the answer to that, in Ireland, is – no. Not so far.

The forces of the bankers and the bondholders, the rich, the Europhiles, the bureaucrats and the political parties are organized and working overtime. Some citizens make their voices known, most wait and hope in silence.

So, the failed policies continue.

To repeat the point Theo Dorgan made on the night of the 2011 election, when Fianna Fáil was hammered: 'People are going through a strange, slow-motion crash of the state . . . They've dealt with one of the great monoliths. They're now scrupulously giving the other monolith in the old politics its shot. And when that proves itself – as it absolutely will, I'm completely certain of this – a busted flush, then the new politics will happen. So it seems to me this is an interim moment in a long, unfolding process of change.'

That's the optimistic view. And we can hope that's how this is playing out. If not, if the old politics linger on, the stagnancy that will follow, and the potential for a carnival of reaction, will be quite beyond anything that ever happened in previous recessions.

Do we bring back Fianna Fáil? Give them another chance, maybe with Labour to hold their hand? Do we push Fianna Fáil and Fine Gael together? Is there any combination of these parties that won't give a large part of its allegiance to bankers, developers and 'our external friends' in the ECB?

Do we tentatively increase the independent, left and Sinn Féin presence at each of the next few elections, as a counterweight? How many more years of austerity, as the old politics tries and retries the old answers, before the real economy is irreparably damaged?

It may well be that it's just too hard to face up to what is happening. There's no mistaking that the citizens are frightened – they want to trust authority figures. So, they wait, they hope.

Those who dissent from the austerity regime are belittled. They're dismissed with a series of questions, and too often they attempt to answer them, thereby allowing the Austerity Hawks to shape the debate.

Well, what would you *cut?*

And how would you *get rid of the deficit?*

And what would you *say when the Troika tell you that you better do what they say or else?*

Such questions should be rejected.

The Austerity Hawks demand that we give answers from a narrow range of options chosen from their view of how the world should be. Accept that, or you're simply 'not serious'.

Those who blew up the credit bubble, guaranteed the dying banks, recapitalized the zombie banks with public money, destroyed the real economy, handed the country over to the ECB, deflated the economy in an effort to expand it and wagged their tails whenever the Troika clicked its fingers, still consider themselves to be 'serious people'.

And those who don't play within the ground rules they set are, of course, unserious people.

Effectively, if we resist austerity policies we're told we must be prepared to write an alternative budget, within the terms forced on Brian Cowen and Brian Lenihan.

Well, to hell with that.

In the years of the frenetic borrowing, anyone who raised questions was shouted down. For the past four years, anyone dissenting from the bank guarantee, from the recapitalization, from the paying of failed bondholders, has been treated as daft. There is, they were solemnly told, no alternative.

We have to face the facts. With their gambling, their phoney boom and their austerity response, they've screwed the country. And this mess will last for years. There's no credible prediction that the mass unemployment, the charges and levies and price rises, will end within the next decade. And the consequences of the mad policies of the last four years are that we'll be paying interest on the bank debt through the years after that.

Official Ireland's austerity strategy takes this recession right off into the far distance. We who dissent from it will not be coming up with any short-term magic bullets.

The choice is between continuing with the mad austerity policies, and the demands of the class warriors – reduce the deficit precisely as the ECB instructs, protect the banks, protect the euro, protect the ECB, maintain the hierarchies of inequality so that the pampered rich will feel incentivized to create jobs.

Or, reject austerity, and all that goes with it. And attempt to re-build a less divided, more sustainable society.

How?

We might lay out a political programme that has as its centre, for example, cutting unemployment, ending forced emigration and a fair unravelling of the personal-debt crisis. To this end we might draw up detailed policies based on the abundant suggestions for change offered by socially minded people over the past four years. Such policies would, of course, be instantly rejected by the Austerity Hawks. Mass unemployment, emigration and unpayable debt are not high on their agenda. They'd like to do something with these things, of course, but none is a priority.

We could – as the left in the Dáil does – call for a Keynesian stimulus programme. And, as the left in the Dáil always does, we could say it should be funded from the National Pension Reserve

Fund. But, of course, the twenty-odd billions of our money saved up in the NPRF has been mostly drained off, to pay bankers' debts.

Anyway, the austerity policies have so weakened the country that there's no guarantee that a Keynesian stimulus would have much effect.

We could use the next general election to demand significant change. But, we know from the 2011 election that they will lie to us, then do as they wish.

We could demand a stiff recession tax on the rich.

We could insist on caps on pay, in both the public and private sectors – enforced through the recession tax – that would greatly reduce the wasteful, divisive inequality.

Since the Austerity Hawks are attacking the severely disabled, and they're whipping supports out from under kids with problems, the dying and the suicidal, they can hardly deny that the country is in a state of emergency. Tough decisions are necessary.

The current top marginal tax rate is 52 per cent. This is spoken of, by the cheerleaders of austerity, as an unwholesome level for rich people to pay. Good God, they'll be so disincentivized. What civilized capitalist country could take so much from the rich?

In the USA, in 1929, the top marginal rate was 24 per cent; then the economy crashed. They put it up to 64 per cent by 1932. In the years that followed, they took seriously the job of fighting the depression and put marginal tax rates for the rich up to 94 per cent. And it stayed at around 90 per cent right up to 1964, when they eased a bit, down to 70 per cent. That was the most sustained era of prosperity for the greatest number of people in American history.

By 1980, when Reagan arrived, the marginal rate for the rich was 50 per cent. When he left eight years later it was 28 per cent. Thus began the bizarre low-tax, light-touch regulation experiment that was Reaganism and Thatcherism.

It ended in 2008, with an almighty crash.

In short, mollycoddling the rich isn't an economic tool to incentivize creative thinking. It's a gift to the rich, from their deep admirers – the politicians and top civil servants of Official Ireland, who want to shape the country in the image of those they admire.

Ah, but these elites will quit rather than lose their rock-star wages.

Fine. Off, you go, folks. The country is falling down with young, capable, energetic people with a stake in the future, not in the accumulated perks and privileges of the past. Sure, they'll make mistakes – but on their worst day they can't possibly do worse than the clowns who've been in charge.

Any society that claims to be fighting a deep recession and maintains low marginal tax rates for the wealthy isn't serious. Cutting services for children, the sick, the dying and the disabled – while sympathizing with bankers on a mere half a million a year – isn't just sick, it's waste we can't afford.

Ah, but sure, if you don't incentivize the rich, sure, they won't create jobs.

Private-sector jobs are created out of market demand. Market demand arises from the disposable income and confidence of the mass of the people. The austerity policies of the past four years have sucked both money and confidence out of the domestic market.

The notion of the rich lone-wolf 'job creator' acting outside of market demand and insisting on extra goodies before he'll sprinkle pixie dust on the economy is a neoliberal fantasy.

Most jobs are created by people running small and medium businesses, knowing their business, knowing their market and reacting to market demand. They see an opportunity to expand or consolidate, they take it. Most such people are citizens, deeply rooted in society. Most such people understand that without jobs and growth and sustained demand there is no future for their business. And measures that promote personal greed at the expense of communal welfare do them no favours.

We could stop the pensions currently being paid to prematurely retired politicians; they should, on reaching sixty-five, get back whatever they paid in. Full stop. One of the major obscenities of this country is the legion of former politicians living easy lives on massive pensions, having destroyed the country. While the rest of us run up debts to pay those pensions.

Reduce TD wages to €60,000. No extra payment for ministers: the job you do when elected, whether as a TD or a minister, has equal value in the democratic process. They should be honoured to have such a job; they don't need big wages, a car and people bowing and scraping to them.

It's not in our interest to protect the hierarchy of greed that Official Ireland insists is a condition of recovery – the absurdly generous wages and fees paid to politicians, professionals and the battalions of useless consultants, the top civil servants and the top grades within the private sector. A tax of 100 per cent could be applied above a certain rate.

Even if we taxed the layers of those on super-incomes, of course, there would be a big gap between income and expenditure. In the long term, that deficit could be brought down by growth, by the natural interaction of supply and demand, an able workforce and available markets. And in the long term we need to decide what kind of country we want. Do we want a country in which significant numbers of people work for decades on low wages, in insecure jobs, and die on hospital waiting lists? Do we want a country in which some people work hard and get minimum wages, and others are paid fantastic amounts because they have a professional title or what some call a 'social status' – well, we've already got that.

In the medium term, there would have to be a reckoning with the ECB.

We need to stop sneering at the Greeks and start making contacts with others suffering the pain of austerity – in Greece, in Portugal, in Spain, in Italy, in the UK. And we need to make a case to the German and French citizens, over the heads of the neoliberals. Reckless austerity threatens their future, too.

Not one more cent for the failed investments of bondholders. The promissory notes? Call the ECB in, tell them we can't afford to pay the billions the bankers lost.

When are we getting back the billions from the National Pension Reserve Fund that were extorted on the direction of the ECB, and squandered on the banks?

When are the billions borrowed in our name, to bail out Irish, German, French and UK bankers, going to be written off? Not a token percentage – the lot.

This would require a fight. As long as the great majority of citizens cling to hope that the old politics offer a way out, we will keep our heads down and take a beating. It's been four years so far. Perhaps after another four, or eight, or twelve.

In the immediate term, there will be no relief from the austerity regime. Right across the globe, the policy has been discredited, but the leaders of Official Ireland believe wholeheartedly in austerity, as much as they still believe in the importance of light-touch regulation.

Perhaps our best bet in the short term is to adopt the same slogan that motivates the wealthy. What we have we hold. Individually, and as a class, they're explicit about maintaining their privileges. It would be over-generous of us not to adopt precisely the same stance.

The first thing we can tell Official Ireland is that we will not take responsibility for cleaning up their mess – but we will set limits to how they go about cleaning up that mess. And that requires defending ourselves against each and every cut.

Not one cent in extra charges, not one cent off any wage or benefit – until each and every unearned privilege is stripped away, until the focus is the interests of the citizens, not the interests of golden circles.

There are some extra taxes on the wider mass of citizens, some cuts, some reforms, that might indeed make sense in a fair society. But as long as the cutting and the taxing is about saving the bankers, as long as it's about preserving privilege and following the ECB agenda, the answer should be no. A society not held to ransom by the failed theology of the old politics could assess its funding needs and tax accordingly, openly, fairly.

Meanwhile, the country continues to function in line with 'the wonderful factor of greed'. Failed developers are given jobs helping NAMA straighten out the mess they made – at salaries up to €200,000 a year. From the courts to the banks to the hospitals to the Financial Centre, professionals continue to rake in extreme fees as though they held some kind of perpetual lottery ticket they were handed along with their professional degree.

At the top of the civil service, the salaries remain huge and the pensions sublime – the performance remains nothing special.

And the unemployed are threatened with losing benefits if they don't train for jobs that don't and won't exist.

The crisis so far is mere prelude. The future is more of the same, with intermittent claims that we've turned the corner, with the economy limping along through 2020.

The biggest lie of them all is the claim that we're all in this together; that we have a common cause in 'waving goodbye to the IMF'; that we are 'sharing the pain' and that we will somehow, some day, share the rewards. Since 2008, this crisis has been all about bankers and banks, bondholders and profits, politicians and their ambitions, EU bureaucrats and their strategies for Europe and the single currency. They want their neoliberal world back.

It's not about the unemployed; it's not about the sick, the elderly. It's not about those who work hard, who fear for their jobs and wages and conditions, who watch their ability to provide for their families being whittled away by the month. It's not about the young, their futures casually thrown away, as the elites struggle to hold onto their privileges.

Without real change, the concerns of the old politics will continue to dominate. Countless middle-aged people will never work again. Wages will continue to be pushed down, working conditions will be trashed. The aged will wallow in need, the young will leave in despair. An old generational pattern of Irish life reasserts itself: we procreate so that they may emigrate.

The bigger picture is simple. For thirty years, a triumphant neo-liberalism operated a debt machine, inventing novel ways to lend money, to sell, to consume – and all the time the solid core of debt was growing and growing until it destabilized the entire structure.

That huge core of debt remains – and, effectively, there isn't enough money in the world to pay it back – but the gamblers who won't accept their own failure are insisting we pick up the tab. And their fans in the dominant political parties believe that's the way to go.

Even if it worked, it would be immoral. And it's not working.

Voices

Sometimes it seems almost as though there's just one voice – the voice of austerity. A chorus of cheerleaders, paid and unpaid, constantly applaud the old politics.

But there have been other voices speaking out from the ranks of the citizens. Four of them are included in the following pages.

These voices are not here to endorse the contents, politics or analysis of this book. They have their own views, their own analysis. They're here because their voices are strong and eloquent expressions of other ways of looking at the crisis. And, in this time of subservience and fear, we desperately need other voices and other ways of looking at what is happening to us.

To the Rising Generation, Amid the Ruins, *by Theo Dorgan*

Theo Dorgan is a poet. This is the speech he gave when addressing graduates of University College Cork at their winter conferring, on 8 December 2010.

YOU, THE RISING GENERATION, face many challenges, but your strength of heart can create a better Ireland.

You come here today to be honoured, as you should be, for your considerable achievements. You come here today to be congratulated, as you should be, for the hard work, self-discipline and sheer good fortune that have brought you to this point in your lives.

Well, I honour you, and I congratulate you, and I wish you continued good fortune in your lives, but it would not be right, it would lack respect, if I were to stand here today before you and utter polite, meaningless words.

A great deal of the country's wealth has been invested in each and every one of you. Your parents have sacrificed much so that you can stand here today and allow them to feel hope for your futures, pride in your achievements. Your teachers have worked hard for you and with you because that is their task, their duty – to pass on to you the knowledge that is the foundation of our culture, our civilization. And you yourselves have already begun to contribute your energies and your insights to our always emerging common good.

These, then, should be days of hope as we stand back to allow you, the rising generation, to begin the great work of building on what has been given you. These should be days of hope when we say to you, Go, you, and do better than we have done, dare more, imagine more, build stronger and deeper and better on the foundations we have laid.

This is as it should be, but our joy and our satisfaction, our pride in your achievements, is shadowed and undermined by the present circumstances.

These are dark days in our broken and battered Republic. Fear is everywhere, fear and bewilderment and uncomprehending rage. The ground is not solid beneath our feet; the way ahead is clouded and uncertain.

None of this is of your making, none of this is your fault, and, if you choose, none of this need be your future responsibility – for you can choose to walk away. Nobody here has the right to blame you if that should be your choice. We have one life and one life only; each man and woman must decide for themselves how and where to live that life.

What faces you, should you choose to stay, should you find yourselves unable or unwilling to leave, is not what anyone here today would have envisaged for you.

This world you are about to inherit is not the world your teachers and parents would have wished for you. Where we should have been building a nation, we surrendered our better selves to the pitiless business of getting and spending. Where we should have been taking thought, considering how to build an economy that would serve a vision of being fully human, we gave ourselves over to the fevered dreams of the prophets of greed. And now we stand in the ruins before a rising generation and we ask ourselves, what has been done here? More pertinently and painfully, what has been done to the children of the nation?

Today, many of you stand ready to play your part in the thankless work of rebuilding our society, our Republic. Many of you have already made plans to leave. Some of you hope to stay but fear you will be forced before long to leave.

How did it come to this? There is no easy answer; I will not insult you by suggesting there is an easy answer.

Ten years ago, this university did me the honour of inviting me to address its graduates and postgraduates on a similar occasion.

Among other things, I said these words:

> We live . . . in a problematic reality now, the variousness
> of what lives and dies only fitfully seen behind the
> lightning clouds of a consumer economy, the music of
> what happens drowned out by the roaring and screeching
> of an economy that has lost the run of itself. This
> Republic has invested time and money and human care in
> your formation, but somehow has lost itself along the way.

I should have listened more closely to myself. I should have paid more attention to what was happening all around me, I should have realized that, ten years ago, we had already lost our Republic. In a republic, we value ourselves, and we value each other. In a republic, it is an honour to serve. In a republic, the highest good is the common good, but in truth we have handed you a fractured state where those who work for the common good have great hearts but little power, and those to whom we entrusted power have betrayed us shamelessly.

I was shaped in this college by women and men who encouraged us to read wisely and reflect well, by men and women who strove to teach us to consider things as they actually are before going on to imagine how things might be, could be, should be.

Well, this is how things actually are:

Our liberties have been trampled on by a professional political class that is as fearful as it is incompetent, perhaps fearful because it is incompetent. Our futures have been mortgaged into the fourth generation to save a corrupt banking system. Those whom we pay to serve us have made slaves of us, and of our children, and of our children's children.

Many, many people refused this reductionist vision; in community-development projects, in hundreds of voluntary organizations, in our own lives, many of us refused – but we were swept away.

It came to the point where, in a time when so many of our young people are taking their own lives, those of us who warned of the coming catastrophe, those of us who were struggling in all good faith to articulate a better way, were invited by the Taoiseach of our country to 'commit suicide'.

We need to reflect on these things calmly, dispassionately, and, having reflected, we must decide among ourselves what is to be done. That task will bear heavily on the shoulders of your generation. That responsibility, if you are brave and generous enough to accept it, will fall to you.

I want to call to mind here something my friend and colleague, the writer Colm Tóibín, said recently: it is not the poets and the singers, the actors and film-makers, musicians, novelists and playwrights who have brought on the present disaster.

I would go further: it is not the teachers and nurses, the chemists and engineers and lawyers, the bus drivers, the factory workers, the shop assistants, the lecturers and security guards, the ambulance drivers and farmers who have brought on the present disaster.

It is not the thousands involved in after-school training of young sportsmen and -women, the tens of thousands who work in and with our charities, the lifeboat volunteers, those who visit the sick and the elderly, those who counsel the homeless, the grief-stricken and the addicted who have brought on the present disaster.

Under the carapace of the state as it imagines itself there is still the nation, troubled, uncertain and beaten down, to be sure, but still struggling to build a civic society.

There is an Ireland we have been ceaselessly imagining and re-imagining for centuries. You can find elements of that Ireland in the thoughts and dreams of Redmond and Pearse, Wolfe Tone and Douglas Hyde. You can find it in the generous vision of James Connolly and the pragmatic vision of that greatest of civil servants, T. K. Whitaker. You can find it in the challenging presidencies of Mary Robinson and Mary McAleese, in the words and deeds of those who fought so trenchantly and fearlessly for the rights of women, the rights of so-called minorities, the rights of the dispossessed.

You can find it in all those who subsumed doubt and difference in the act of faith that is the Belfast Agreement. You can find it in the words of our poets and writers, the visions of our artists, the soul-building songs and music of both the dead and the living generations.

Many of us live fragments of that Ireland in our daily lives; much of that Ireland we have already brought into being – but we have failed to imagine clearly enough the civic and political structures that will nurture and grow and guarantee our visions of the good.

That is our task now, that is the task you face – if you are prepared, as I hope in my heart you are prepared, to accept the responsibility.

But we live and die as individuals and your first responsibility is to yourself, to the life you have been mysteriously granted. For myself, I will honour whatever choice you make, I will wish you well if you stay or if you go.

If you must go, then go with a full heart and high expectations of the world. Do not go in defeat, with regret, in loneliness. We live in one world now, infinitely various, full of undiscovered joys and surprises. Savour your lives and remember you have a nation still, a home to return to. When you come back, bring us what you have learned in the wide world as thousands of immigrants are already enriching us with the learning they bring to our homes and to our streets. Send us your visions and thoughts constantly; it's what the technology is for. You will be elsewhere, not orphaned or cast out. You can elect, I hope you will elect, to remain a part of the national conversation, a part of our evolution towards a better life for all.

And if you stay? I say, You have the same opportunities to learn and explore, to discover and innovate, to be surprised and joyful, to learn and to help teach us all what it is to be fully human.

What we must learn now, what we must practise with all our minds and hearts, is solidarity. Wherever we are, no matter how cast down: solidarity. No matter how grim the circumstances, how seemingly hopeless the situation: solidarity. At all times, among all peoples: solidarity. Solidarity, and hope.

As far back as the sixth century BC, the Greek poet Theognis of Megara said: 'Hope is the one good god remaining.'

Hope is a profound act of imagination, the most important and the most neglected of the civic virtues. In the face of the present disaster we can lie down in despair, or we can choose hope – which means placing all our faith in each other and in the boundless capacity of the imagination to reinvent circumstance, to establish new truths.

We are no mean people, as Yeats said in another place, in another context. We have hearts and minds, we care for each other still, we have our dreams and, in dreams, as the poet Delmore Schwartz once said, in dreams begin responsibilities. It falls to you, to your generation, to assume the responsibility of dreaming a new republic.

The nation is beaten down, but not defeated. A certain kind of Ireland is over and we are well rid of it. There is a new Ireland to be imagined and worked for, a new kind of Ireland to build, and it is you who must build it. Everything I have seen of this rising generation persuades me of your strength of heart and it is heart we need now, the heart steadied and strengthened by the mind and by the power of imagination.

May your hearts continue strong, may your lives be long and fruitful, may your most generous and courageous visions come to pass.

The Ballyhea Theses, *by the Ballyhea/Charleville Marchers*

It's been a feature of this recession that Irish citizens meekly accepted what was done to them. We accepted cuts in services, one charge piled upon another, with only token complaint. It's true, but it's not the whole truth.

Students, carers, the parents of vulnerable children all raised their own protests, albeit in isolation. One remarkable protest went to the heart of the indignity being heaped on the citizens – the imposition of huge amounts of debt, in order to pay the failed gambles of bond-holders.

Week after week, from March 2011, citizens of Ballyhea and Charleville, in north Cork, marched each Sunday in a sustained and dignified protest against the forced payment of bank bondholders. They were supporters of the mainstream parties, and supporters of none. Just citizens outraged by what was being done. The Ballyhea Says No protest made an unanswerable case against the debt-and-austerity policies of the government.

In June 2012, fifteen of the Ballyhea/Charleville marchers

travelled to Frankfurt. There, in imitation of the protest in 1517 by Martin Luther, who nailed his Ninety-five Theses to the castle church at Wittenberg, they Blu-tacked their own theses 'to the door of one of the new churches of European society – in fact to its very cathedral, the head office of the ECB'.

The document was a concise summing-up of the burden to which the country had been subjected. This is what it said.

TODAY, JUNE 6TH 2012, NEARLY five hundred years on from Martin Luther's stand on October 31st 1517, when, 'Out of love for the truth and the desire to bring it to light' he nailed his famous protest, his *95 Theses*, to the door of the castle church at Wittenberg in Germany, we've come from Ireland – from Ballyhea, from Charleville, from a few other areas – and we're on a similar mission.

We don't have 95 Theses, we do have a righteous cause and we do have our own protests, our own Theses:

1)   Why has the ECB never accepted blame for its own negligence in oversight since the launch of the euro?

2)   The euro was an incomplete currency from creation, lacking in the kind of centralized control mechanisms enjoyed by such as the dollar, pound, yen, etc.; in those circumstances the ECB should have been extra-vigilant – it wasn't.

3)   In the early and mid-2000s a tidal wave of hundreds of billions of cheap euro flooded out from the private banks at the core of Europe, in France and Germany especially, and swamped the economies of those countries on the periphery; the ECB ignored every warning sign.

4)   When the bubble burst in Ireland, in 2008, our national debt stood at less than €50 billion, our National Pension Reserve Fund at just under €20 billion, so in effect we were less than €30 billion in the red.

5)   We did have a problem, a budget deficit that year of €13.1 billion – large, but not insurmountable if tackled with decisiveness and courage.

6)   Nearly five years of austerity budgets later our national debt stands at nearly €170 billion and rapidly heading for €200 billion, our National Pension Reserve Fund has been raided to the tune of €17 billion, stands at just over €5 billion (it had grown during 2008/09/10), which means we're in the red to the tune of about €165 billion, an eight-fold increase. Our budget deficit for this year will be over €14 billion, which means that despite all that austerity, all that massively increased national debt, we're *still* no further forward in that most vital area.

7)   The reason we are now many times worse off than when all this began? We've been bailing out the bank bondholders. One fateful weekend in September 2008 top representatives of the Irish banks met with top members of the government, presented them with a doomsday situation, secured a two-year blanket guarantee of all their deposits and liabilities; they did so while offering incomplete/false/misleading information, so that the then Finance Minister Brian Lenihan boasted that it would cost 'only' €5 billion.

8)   Gradually the true picture emerged and, since then, to mid-April 2012 (per current Finance Minister Michael Noonan), the Irish banks have paid out over €103 billion in bonds.

9)   In that time, we – the Irish people – have committed €67.8 billion to the Irish banks (€62.8 billion per Minister Noonan again, a further €5 billion through NAMA), with talk now that they will require a further €4 billion in the next year or two; this in a country whose GDP at the moment is at around €160 billion.

10)   The bulk of that commitment has been at the behest of the

ECB, which has used its financial muscle – cheap funding to our Central Bank – to blackmail successive Irish governments into assuming for the Irish people a debt that is not ours.

11) Those bank bonds were private deals between consenting adults in private for-profit institutions, deals done under the prevailing fundamental rule of commerce – 'WARNING: your investment can fall as well as rise.' The lending institutions fully understood that warning but, blinded by the potential profits, heedless of the bubble building in Ireland, they plunged in anyway.

12) When the Irish banks failed those bonds failed with them; under that fundamental rule of commerce, of capitalism, those bondholders should then have taken their hit, their haircut. Enter the ECB, and its blackmail policy as applied to Ireland.

13) The ECB feared contagion if the Irish banks didn't pay their bondholders, the risk of collapse to the big banks at Europe's core in Germany and France – who had huge exposure to massive loans made to all the at-risk countries – and thence to the euro itself.

14) Since these were ECB fears, then the ECB itself should have assumed the responsibility for those bonds, and it had the capacity to do so.

15) Instead, the ECB has forced that responsibility on to Ireland, which – as evidenced in the numbers above – does NOT have the capacity to carry it.

16) So we ask, by what right do you do this to us? To echo Martin Luther's Thesis 86 – *Why does the pope, whose wealth today is greater than the wealth of the richest Crassus, build the basilica of St Peter with the money of poor believers rather than with his own money?* – we ask: Why does the ECB, whose wealth today is greater than the wealth of the richest Crassus, pay

the bank bondholders with the money of poor believers rather than with its own money?

17) What are the ethical, moral, legal or even logical grounds for what you are doing to Ireland? You have spoken often and loudly of the 'moral hazard' effect if Ireland doesn't pay for the recklessness of its bankers; what of the 'moral hazard' effect on the bondholders, whose own recklessness doesn't just go unpunished but is actually fully rewarded?

18) How do you explain your unprecedented interference in the course of commerce, your corruption of the one of the basic laws of capitalism, that of profit and loss?

19) Before there can be any borrower, reckless or otherwise, there has to be a lender; why is it that under your edicts those who so recklessly loaned hundreds of billions not just into Ireland but also into Greece, Italy, Spain, Portugal are themselves the last and the least to suffer?

20) In 2010 you 'allowed' the Irish Central Bank to print an additional €30.7 billion to enable two zombie banks to pay failed bonds, the infamous Promissory Notes as collateral; not a cent of that €30.7 billion went to the Irish people: why should we now be made liable for even a cent of it?

21) Since this crisis began your management of it has been abysmal; despite all your measures, all your meetings, not alone has it never gotten even a whit better, it has gone from bad to worse to catastrophic.

22) We call on you to admit to your own mistakes, to your own negligence from day one of the creation of the euro right up to the present moment.

23) We call on you to rethink everything you're doing, not just to change course but to reverse course and start again.

24) We call on you to write off the Promissory Notes in their entirety, to write off the bank debt you have already forced

on us, the Irish people, and to do with those banks what you should have done from day one – assume responsibility for them yourselves.

25) This started life as the European Coal and Steel Community (ECSC), became the European Economic Community (EEC), then the EU.

26) In a genuine community the strong help the weak; in this community you – the strong – have taken advantage of the weakness and vulnerability of one of the smallest countries in the EU and forced debt on us that is not ours.

27) Over the years we've had the addition of the European Parliament, the European Commission, the Council of the European Union, the European Council, the Court of Justice of the European Union, and the European Central Bank, layer on layer of administration.

28) The most significant of those, however, has been the formation of your own institution, the ECB, in 1998. Since 1998 the ECB has been growing ever more powerful, to the stage where it is now beginning to dictate even to the elected representatives in Europe.

29) The proposed ESM [European Stability Mechanism] treaty, as written, gives even more powers to the bankers and financiers, powers unprecedented in any democracy anywhere, ever – powers unprecedented in any kind of jurisdiction, even in the likes of the USSR or North Korea.

30) The proposed ESM treaty as written not only puts anyone who ever works for it beyond the law, it puts any document it ever writes, any decision it ever makes, any building it ever occupies, beyond even investigation – total immunity for itself and anyone associated with it.

31) This will enable it to do whatever it pleases with absolute impunity and with total immunity. The original aims and

values of the European project have been lost; we are now fast heading for a new superpower – the EUB, European Union of Bankers.

32) All the diagnoses made by the ECB of this crisis have been wrong, all the prescriptions have failed – in fact, they've made the situation worse.

33) It's time to stop, it's time to reconsider this whole project, it's time the ECB were brought to account. Just as the Catholic Church was a dominant power in Europe five hundred years ago, the ECB has become a dominant force today. Omnipotence, however, doesn't mean they're always right, doesn't mean they should not be challenged. In time, and just as the Catholic Church came to see that what it was doing then was wrong, so people will see that what the ECB is doing now to Ireland and to other sovereign peoples across Europe is wrong.

34) And so, our challenge.

Signed this day, June 6th 2012:

Pat O'Brien   *Cathleen Moloney*
Frances O'Brien   *Pat Moloney*
Fiona Buckley   *Diarmaid Ó Cadhla*
Rob Buckley   *Donncha Ó Briain*
Richard Chapman   *Lynette O'Donoghue*
Vicky Donnelly   *Diarmuid O'Flynn*
Hugh Mellerick   *Phil Ryan*
Damian Moylan

I'm Tired of Saying Nothing and I'm Tired of being Afraid,
by Evelyn O'Connor

This is the full text of the speech delivered by Evelyn O'Connor, of Mount St Michael Secondary School, Claremorris, Mayo, on her receipt of the Secondary School Teacher of the Year Award, in June 2012. Her words are about teachers: the speech could equally apply to other groups disrespected and belittled by those who seek to divide us.

THE VERY FIRST THING I want to say is: 'Thanks, lads.'

This isn't going to turn into an Oscar acceptance speech – but I do genuinely want to thank those of you who nominated me, both those who I teach here in this building and those who belong to my virtual classroom online.

I am grateful for this award and I am proud of the part my students played in helping me achieve it.

As an English teacher I always tell ye to try to avoid clichés but you'll have to allow me this one:

I love teaching. And I know that I am very privileged to have a job that I love.

One reason why I love my job is because I believe that teachers can and do make a difference in students' lives – I had a teacher who made all the difference to me.

My English teacher's name was Mrs Freeley. She's the reason that I became a teacher and one of the most important things she taught me was that it's okay to be a rebel.

She would have been very proud of me today but sadly she's not here any more, she died last Christmas Eve.

It's pretty ironic, to me, that as I'm receiving this award for Teacher of the Year, I have no idea if I'll have a job in a year's time.

As you know, I am not a permanent member of staff.

Two English teachers had just retired when I started teaching here; and I went through a rigorous interview process competing to get this job. Another English teacher, Ms Shallow, retired this year but the contract I'm about to sign will effectively deny me a secure future in this school because of a bizarre bureaucratic nightmare.

The school wants me here. You the students seem to want me here. And I want to be here.

If I go to a different school – which I don't want to do – I have to start my career all over again. And even though I've been teaching for nine years, it'll be at least another five years before I qualify for any kind of job security.

Now I haven't told you my story because I think I'm special or perfect – I'm not. I make mistakes. And I'm not trying to get my story out there because I think I'm special.

I've become visible because I created a useful website that students all over the country are using but I'm just a regular teacher, who more than anything wants to teach. And there are so, so many non-permanent teachers up and down the country in the same position as me.

The government want us and the public to believe that they haven't cut the pupil–teacher ratio, but this is a carefully crafted illusion.

- They have taken away the allowance for career-guidance teachers.
- They have taken away the hours which were granted to schools who run the Leaving Cert Vocational Programme.
- They have abolished language support for non-nationals and reduced special-needs hours or made them non-supernumerary.
- And they have introduced a redeployment system which means that those who are already in the system can be moved around like pawns on a chessboard and those of us who are non-permanent are non-existent.

Every time a teacher is redeployed – in most cases against their wishes – a non-permanent teacher loses their job.

It seems that in our new low-cost education system, all teachers are equal, but some teachers are more equal than others.

If I sound like I'm running for election, I apologize. God knows the last thing this country needs is another teacher in the Dáil. I don't want to be a politician, I just want to teach.

If you are wondering why non-permanent teachers aren't screaming about this from the rooftops – the simple answer is because we are afraid.

Teachers aren't popular in this country.

We are afraid to even say these things out loud because the government will try to use our complaints as an excuse to make things even worse for all teachers.

We're afraid that if we make ourselves visible we might lose our jobs. We're afraid that people will dismiss us as whingers because of our summer holidays.

When people looked at me enviously when we finished up a few weeks ago I didn't know what to say to them.

I didn't tell them about the ball of anxiety in my stomach [because of] wondering if my contract would be renewed; wondering how many hours I'd be granted for next year; wondering if my family and I should just abandon Ireland and set up home somewhere else. I become like Hamlet: I know that 'it is not nor it cannot come to good but break my heart for I must hold my tongue'.

Well, I'm tired of saying nothing and I'm tired of being afraid. Non-permanent teachers have to stop going quietly because our students and our schools are suffering. And because my English teacher once taught me that it was right to rebel against stupidity and injustice.

The department aren't interested in my situation or in our school's difficulties. Schools are a maths equation to them. If you have your quota of allocated teachers to pupils then you just have to make it work somehow.

Well, I have an exam question for the Education Minister Ruairi Quinn. If he would like to take the time to come down here and tell us exactly how it's possible to timetable 475 pupils for English with just two permanent teachers he is more than welcome.

The Project Maths teachers would be delighted because this is the kind of real-world problem the minister insists he wants students to get to grips with.

Of course, sadly we know that Ruairi Quinn has no intention of paying us a visit. Both he and our Taoiseach Enda Kenny were invited to attend these awards weeks ago, long before the judges made their decision. They both declined.

The irony of this isn't lost on me either. No one in power seems in the slightest bit interested in encouraging, celebrating and recognizing good teaching. Their solution would most likely be to redeploy someone else into my job and leave me on the dole.

And believe me I know right now there are hundreds of thousands of highly capable and qualified people in this country who are unemployed. My husband is one of them. But if you have children, if you care about education, you should want the hundreds of teachers up and down the country who are losing their jobs to be kept in the system.

In this country we are very proud of our national sports, hurling and football.

But as a teacher for nearly a decade I would humbly propose we add teacher-bashing to this list.

It's a measure I suppose of the passion Irish people have for education that nothing irritates us more than a teacher who we feel is unfit to teach.

I have a three-year-old daughter and I'd like to think that the people who are entrusted to educate her for the next fifteen years will be good at what they do and will take it seriously.

But despite our national obsession with criticizing teachers, I need to point out that the majority of teachers in this country *are* good at what they do and *do* take it seriously.

And when my daughter, Hazel, goes to school that doesn't mean that I'll agree with every decision her teachers make; it doesn't mean that I'll necessarily agree with their style of teaching.

Crucially it doesn't mean that I can measure the effectiveness of what teachers do by looking at exam results.

They've tried this in the UK and America and it has completely undermined teachers, students and education to the extent that most teachers leave the profession within three years.

Measuring teacher effectiveness by exam results only aggravates the problem of 'teaching to the test' instead of offering students a real education, and this is a problem that we are already all too familiar with in this country.

What I'd really like for us to do as a country, though, is to have a different conversation. A positive conversation.

Let's talk about good teaching. My whole life, people – parents, friends, college lecturers, even fellow teachers – have tried to persuade me that I'm wasting my talents being a teacher. But why can't being a teacher be as prestigious as being a doctor? A good doctor saves people. A good teacher inspires them.

The fact of the matter is, if we want teachers to be proud of, we need to make it a profession you would be proud to be part of.

Instead of attacking teachers and tearing their morale to shreds we should be asking, what makes a good teacher? And what makes a good teacher great?

We should ask, how can we keep attracting good teachers to the profession? How can we stop them from leaving teaching? And how can we help our teachers to get better at what they do?

And we should, of course, ask, what about our students? What do you want to learn? How do you want to learn? Do you want to learn? And what can we do to make this happen?

We should also try to figure out the working conditions that make it possible for people to become the best teachers they can possibly be. I teach over two hundred pupils. How can I possibly give all of them the individual attention they need?

Why do you think I argue so passionately against cutbacks? Is it because I'm lazy? Or is it because cutbacks make me worse at my job through no fault of my own?

The reason grinds are so popular in this country isn't because the teachers are rubbish – who do you think are giving the grinds?

It's because the ideal pupil–teacher ratio is 1:1.

We've known this since Socrates taught Plato and he taught Aristotle and he in turn taught Alexander the Great.

When we elected this government they proclaimed – and I'm going to quote here because, as an English teacher, I'm a fan of quotes – that *even in our country's crisis, we can make progress in education and protect frontline services'*. They promised to *'recruit, train and support the highest calibre of teachers'*.

Well, I don't feel very supported and nor do the talented and experienced teachers up and down the country whose jobs are disappearing.

Not to mention the new entrants to the profession who, thanks to pay cuts, will become like second-class citizens in our staffrooms.

I guess what I'm asking now is if the government mean it when they talk about supporting good teachers, or is it just more double-speak?

Obviously, I have a personal agenda here – I want to save my job. But I don't have a political agenda.

My grandfather was a proud Fine Gaeler and I have many friends in the Labour Party.

I want to believe that Fine Gael and Labour can find a way to be better than the idiots who got us into this mess in the first place.

Some positive things are happening in education: our minister Ruairi Quinn is determined to bring about changes in our in-many-ways antiquated educational system – and for this I admire him.

The proposals for the new Junior Cert have the potential to bring about real and meaningful change (but the department need to listen to the teachers), and this is a change I want to be a part of.

But we need to make sure we're making things better not worse. Destroying the morale of the teachers who will be implementing this change is not the way forward.

Minister Quinn will no doubt throw his hands in the air and say there is no money.

Well, I say to Ruairi Quinn and the Department of Education, if this is the limit of your creativity, imagination and passion to protect our children's education – shame on you.

Finally, I want to apologize to my students.

I should be putting every ounce of my energy, my passion and my enthusiasm into my teaching and your learning next year.

Instead I'll be battling with the department, trying to force them to recognize that I am needed in this school.

I'll be distracted from doing my best for you by the fear that someone else will be parachuted into my job and by the fear I will have to consider emigrating to support my family and to continue doing the job that I love.

And for this I apologize. You, our students, deserve better.

The Denials of Possibility,
by Anthony Cronin

Anthony Cronin is a poet and writer. This piece was published in the
Sunday Independent *of 2 January 2011.*

T HE IRELAND IN WHICH I was brought up was a dull, narrow,
restrictive place. The concept of the entrepreneur was un-
known. Those who had money were almost all a tight-fisted lot.
They put their profits in banks, which exported them to England,
which in turn exported them to places like Uruguay at exorbitant
interest rates to build railways. To use a phrase of the time, there
wasn't 'a shillin' stirring'.

Perhaps for that reason, for such things do not thrive in a more
active, ebullient economic environment, pietism and hypocrisy
were the dominant notes struck by officialdom, lay and clerical.
As Frank O'Connor said in a contribution to this newspaper, so
far from a terrible beauty having been born, a terrible boredom
reigned. In the midst of desolation, politicians mouthed patriotic

slogans. Everywhere there was talk of our souls, but the activities by which the spirit really lives – art, literature, and social camaraderie of all kinds – were either starved for sustenance, actively censored or simply forbidden.

I do not want those days to come again. But I know that if the appalling vista of crippling repayments, starved growth, and emigration of the brightest and best continues for too long they will come again. Or if not them, another version of despair which will be even worse: the jackboot of the infallible leader.

Certainly we must get the deficits straightened out. And, but for the great brains of capitalism which agreed at their G20 conference in Canada a year and a half ago that everybody must do it at the same time – a crazy notion – we could have done it without permanent and lasting damage. But repayment of the debts that were incurred by a delinquent banking system and a few favoured customers is another matter. The repayment of those debts could take long enough to return us to something like the dead Ireland of my youth.

But there is a note of hope, albeit of a strange order. This is the deep sense of grievance being felt at the moment, and one that is justified. As the debts pile up, as billions more are tossed into the banks almost every week without so much as a by-your-leave, and while decades of austerity to come loom out of the fog of official jargon as the single undeniable fact, the Irish people are more and more beginning to wonder, to despair and to resent keeping the whole staggering game going. They will have to be told more often and in ever sterner tones that they brought it all upon themselves. But they will not believe that. Quite properly, they do not believe it now and they are still less likely to believe it in a decade or more from now.

The analogy is what happened after the First World War. When the fighting ended the victors found that, so far from having spoils to divide, they themselves owed billions to the Americans and to the world banking system. So they decided to get it all out of the Germans. But the Germans would not pay unless they were forced to admit full responsibility for having brought the war about. So, as part of the settlement, they had to sign a paper admitting such responsibility and promising to repay. They signed, but they didn't believe it. Naturally, after a while the repayments broke down and eventually Hitler came along and tore up that bit of paper as well as all the other bits that were lying around.

In our case, too, a breakdown forcing, at the least, serious negotiation on all the creditors and bondholders involved is by no means off the cards. Take someone who is now just about to leave school. In seven or eight years, when he or she is in their mid-twenties and wants all the substantial things in life that people in their mid-twenties are expected and encouraged to want, when the rest of the world has moved into growth or even boom mode and Ireland is being left out, are they going to face into yet another austerity budget with its threats to jobs and everything else because they feel they have to pay for the sins of the fathers? And all the more so if they have been told by their fathers that there were no sins and it was all because of a small class of people who were carried away by greed and the psychology of the bubble?

But imagine trying to explain it all to a still younger generation who weren't even alive when the onerous debts which will be still being repaid were contracted: Well, there was this man called Seanie, you see, who gave out a lot of money. – To everybody? – Not to everybody. Only to his friends. – Where did he get the money? – From German banks. – And we have to pay it back? – We've been paying it back for a long time now. – And why didn't the people he gave it to pay it back? – Well, they had built all those big empty buildings, you see, all over the place and they gave the rest of it to their wives . . .

When finally things reach crisis point a delegation led by Pearse Doherty, the new Taoiseach, will go to Brussels. They will be prepared for hard bargaining but they will find our creditors are ready to talk. Capitalism needs customers, and Ireland, along with Portugal, Spain, Italy and Greece, has not been a customer for some time. There have been hardly any Mercedes sold here, even to government ministers. Our creditors will be prepared to say the Irish 'cannot' pay instead of 'will not' pay. 'Cannot' looks much better than 'will not' in these cases and so things will be put on the long finger, a very long finger, and at very low interest rates.

The easiest way for a country to get money is to print it, which the US is now doing to a band playing. The second-best way is, I suppose, to earn it. Where countries are concerned, earning more is called growth. Growth is brought about by bright ideas, hard graft, and working capital. The Irish have plenty of bright ideas and they are known and liked all over the world for their ability to combine hard work and a cheerful disposition. Other nationalities who work hard can only do it dourly and with the light of determination in their eye. But the Irish do not have working capital any more. Just as they didn't have it in the Twenties, Thirties, Forties and Fifties. And there aren't any banks prepared to lend it to them. According to the theory favoured by the Department of Finance, the collapse of AIB would have been systemic, that is it would have led to the collapse of all other banks. But, as we know, the whole banking system has in effect collapsed anyway, although we even kept Anglo on life support at preposterous cost. Our banks no longer lend money to us, we lend it to them.

It is all a terrible pity. Money, as we know, does not create happiness. But it does create possibilities. In former years I used to think that the worst thing about Ireland was the denials of possibility. It may be that those denials must come again. But let them not be long sustained.

Acknowledgements

This book was Eoin McHugh's idea, and he has been supportive throughout, as has editor Brian Langan. The production people at Transworld have shown remarkable patience.

Nothing I do would be possible without the support of Julie Lordan, and that was especially true over the past few months.

Theo Dorgan, the Ballyhea/Charleville marchers, Evelyn O'Connor and Anthony Cronin kindly agreed to allow me reproduce the pieces in the 'Voices' section at the end of the book. Thanks to all.

Through the Celtic Bubble period, and the crash, I've had the job of writing the *Sunday Independent's* Soapbox column – under the editorship of the late Aengus Fanning and then under his partner and successor Anne Harris. Willie Kealy has been my immediate boss, advisor and occasionally sceptical listener throughout. This book owes a debt to them and to that column – since about 2006, in particular, it required constant reading of a range of specialist economics writings in print and online, as well as following the daily and weekly business media. Not my favourite reading matter, and I still wince at my limitations. But that world has forced its attentions on the rest of us, in a destructive way, and the record of the expert interpreters of such material is questionable.

Thanks to the *Sunday Independent* reader who alerted me to the St Colmcille quote. To comedian Chris Coltrane for the use of his tweet. And to Lord Gnome's representative, Susan Roccelli.

Sources

The notes below are far from exhaustive, but they attempt to indicate the range of sources to which I'm indebted.

Online, in a world wherein the jargon of economists seems designed to exclude most of us, the clarity and sense of Michael Taft's Notes on the Front blog (*notesfromthefront.typepad.com*) stands out. The Irish Economy blog (*irisheconomy.ie*), the Tasc website and blog Progressive Economy (*progressive-economy.ie*) and Cormac McCabe's Dublin Opinion blog (*dublinopinion.com*) regularly provide instructive data. Life After Nama (*lifeafternama. wordpress*) and Namawinelake (*namawinelake.wordpress.com*) explore specialized matters with as little jargon as possible.

And, for a day-to-day window on the foolishness of Austerity Ireland's leaders and cheerleaders, Broadsheet.ie manages the difficult trick of being both serious and funny.

Among the books to which I returned again and again, to check figures and dates and to understand the background to what's been happening, several stand out. *The Corporate Takeover of Ireland*, by Kieran Allen, *The FitzPatrick Tapes*, by Tom Lyons and Brian

Carey, *Sins of the Father*, by Conor McCabe, and *Towards a Second Republic*, by Peadar Kirby and Mary P Murphy. *Unhealthy State*, by Maev-Ann Wren, a monumental work of journalism, was published five years before the crash, but its examination of the consolidation of a two-tier health service told us much about the dangerous mindset of the Irish elites.

Books

Meltdown: the End of the Age of Greed, by Paul Mason, Verso, 2009.

Why It's Kicking Off Everywhere, by Paul Mason, Verso, 2012.

The Gods That Failed, by Larry Elliot, Dan Atkinson, Vintage, 2009.

Treasure Islands, by Nicholas Shaxson, Vintage 2012.

The Making of the Celtic Tiger, by Ray MacSharry and Padraic White, Mercier 2000.

The Celtic Tiger, by Kieran Allen, Manchester University Press, 2000.

After the Celtic Tiger, by Peter Clinch, Frank Convery and Brendan Walsh, O'Brien Press, 2002.

Unhealthy State, by Maev-Ann Wren, New Island Books, 2003.

Something Rotten, by Simon Carswell, Gill & Macmillan, 2006.

The Corporate Takeover of Ireland, by Kieran Allen, Irish Academic Press, 2007.

The Builders, by Frank McDonald and Kathy Sheridan, Penguin, 2008.

Ireland's Economic Crash, by Kieran Allen, The Liffey Press, 2009.

Who Really Runs Ireland, by Matt Cooper, Penguin, 2009.

Ship of Fools by Fintan O'Toole, Faber and Faber, 2010.

Showtime: The Inside Story of Fianna Fáil in Power, by Pat Leahy, Penguin, 2010.

How Ireland Really Went Bust, by Matt Cooper, Penguin, 2011.

The Bankers by Shane Ross, Penguin, 2010.

Sins of the Father, by Conor McCabe, The History Press, 2011.

Towards a Second Republic, by Peadar Kirby and Mary P Murphy, Pluto Press, 2011.

The FitzPatrick Tapes: The Rise and Fall of One Man, One Bank and One Country, by Brian Carey and Tom Lyons, Penguin 2011.

Bust: How the Courts Have Exposed the Rotten Heart of the Irish Economy, by Dearbhail McDonald, Penguin, 2011.

Anglo Republic: Inside the Bank that Broke Ireland, by Simon Carswell, Penguin, 2011.

Media

Part One: How the Old Politics Brought the Country to Its Knees

'The Million Pound Round', *Scottish Daily Record*, 13 July 2000.

'Woods you pay £1.4m to play with a Tiger?' Lynne Kelleher and Vivienne Aikan, *The Mirror*, 13 July 2000.

'Billionaire Wins Bid For Golf', Hunki Yun, *Orlando Sentinel*, 14 July 2000.

'Pity About the Pint, Tiger', Tim Glover, *Sunday Independent*, 16 July 2000.

Chris de Burgh quotes: from an interview with fan club magazine the *Getaway Gazette*, quoted on cdeb.com, Mr de Burgh's official website.

'Big Swingers: Forget opera – the new corporate Establishment is on the golf course', Chris Blackhurst, *Management Today*, 1 October 2001.

Francis Fukuyama quote: 'The End of History?', *The National Interest* magazine, summer 1989, reprinted at http://www.wesjones.com/eoh.htm

Meltdown, by Paul Mason.

Why It's Kicking Off Everywhere, by Paul Mason.

The Gods That Failed, by Larry Elliot, Dan Atkinson.

Paul Davidson, 'Keynes's Serious Monetary Theory': http://econ.as.nyu.edu/docs/IO/8801/

The quote from the movie *Wall Street*, and the quote from the Ivan Boesky speech on which the movie quote was based, are on IMDB.com.

Sean FitzPatrick 'we discovered just how good we were': *Irish Times*, 22 September 2005.

'The Irish Economic Boom: Facts, Causes and Lessons', Pierre Fortin, Université du Québec à Montréal and Canadian Institute for Advanced Research, December 2000.

The Making of the Celtic Tiger, by Ray MacSharry and Padraic White.

The Celtic Tiger, by Kieran Allen.

After the Celtic Tiger, by Peter Clinch, Frank Convery and Brendan Walsh.

The World Top Incomes Database, website by F. Alvaredo, T. Atkinson, T. Piketty and E. Saez, Paris School of Economics.

Mary Harney and *Morning Ireland*: quoted in 'Be wary about Mary's economic advice', Gene Kerrigan, *Sunday Independent*, 11 November 2001.

'Legend of Charlie "No Strokes" McCreevy', Gene Kerrigan, *Sunday Independent*, 25 July 2004.

Ernst & Young advert: quoted on William Wall's blog, williamwall.net, 7 September 2010.

'Eircom shareholders angry over bonuses', by Sophie Barker, *Daily Telegraph*, 29 August 2000.

Eircom privatisation – quotes and figures from various newspaper reports, and from *Learning From the Eircom Debacle*, published Spring 2011, by the Irish Congress of Trade Unions.

'Mea culpa, I've bunged Fianna Fáil', Gene Kerrigan, *Sunday Independent*, 24 March 2002.

George Lee quote: RTÉ News, 24 March 2000.

'Vroom-vroom' quote: Una McCaffrey, *The Irish Times*, 2 July 2004.

'Investors Use Irish Firms to Hide Money', Siobhan Creaton, *The Irish Times*, 6 February 1998.

'Glaring prejudice on the part of the establishment' quote: Committee of Public Accounts, *Third Interim Report for 2003*, Committee hearings October 2004 to July 2005.

Treasure Islands, by Nicholas Shaxson.

'For Insurance Regulators, Trails Lead to Dublin', Brian Lavery and Timothy L. O'Brien, *New York Times*, 1 April 2005.

Dermot Desmond 'parasitical' quote: *Out on Their Own*, by Ivor Kenny, Gill & Macmillan, 1991.

'Knight Capital Says Trading Glitch Cost It $440 Million': Nathaniel Popper, *New York Times*, 2 August 2012.

Description of bank managers as 'faintly dim former rugby players': 'Ireland's future depends on breaking free from bailout', Morgan Kelly, *Irish Times*, 5 May 2011.

Mitsubishi Trust motorcycle escort: *The Making of the Celtic Tiger*, Ray MacSharry and Padraic White.

Tadashi Kohno quote: *Sins of the Father*, by Conor McCabe, The History Press, 2011.

Michael Gass quote: 'Spitzer rides into town', Joe Brennan and Brian Carey, *Sunday Times*, 24 April 2005.

'Shadow Regulation and the Shadow Banking System', Jim Stewart, Tax Justice Focus, Volume 4, Number 2, 2008.

'Speech by Commissioner Charlie McCreevy on the integration of Europe's financial markets and international cooperation', Euro Conference, New York, 20 April 2005.

'Keynote address by Jean-Claude Trichet', at the Whitaker lecture organized by the Central Bank and Financial Services Authority of Ireland, Dublin, 31 May 2004.

Dale Tussing and Maev-Ann Wren, *How Ireland Cares*, New Island Books, 2006.

Kieran McGrath quote on child care crisis: *Irish Independent*, July 2000 – quoted in *Sunday Independent*, 16 July 2000.

Maev-Ann Wren, *Unhealthy State*.

Brendan Gleeson on *Late Late Show*, www.rte.ie/tv/footer_late-late/20060317

Brian Lenihan on 'not rushing into the banks': 19 November 2008, RTÉ Six One News – quoted in TheStory.ie, 'Talking Points in Time'.

Part Two: The Slow Death of the Old Politics

Theo Dorgan quotes, RTÉ, *The Eleventh Hour*, 25 February 2011.

'Cowen vows to write 'any cheque' to rescue banks', Paul O'Brien, *Irish Examiner*, 15 July 2009.

Brian Cowen quote: 'We're not fucking nationalizing Anglo': in *Showtime: The Inside Story of Fianna Fáil in Power*, by Pat Leahy.

'Maybe we deserve an idiot in Finance', Gene Kerrigan, *Sunday Independent*, 14 September 2008.

'Now it's time to play the blame game', Gene Kerrigan, *Sunday Independent*, 5 October 2008.

'People "went mad" borrowing during boom – Taoiseach', *Irish Independent*, 26 January 2012.

'Public to blame for economic collapse', Anita Guidera, *Irish Independent*, 21 July 2009.

Sean FitzPatrick 'we had the balls' speech: *Irish Times*, 22 September 2005.

Jim Tunney in Brussels: *Private Eye*, issue 247, 4 June 1971.

Jürgen Stark and Jörg Asmussen quotes, *Four Corners*, 'Dicing With Debt', ABC1 television, Australia, reporter Marian Wilkinson, broadcast 12 March 2012.

'Took one for the Euro team' *Business and Finance*, Editor's Blog, 6 December 2011.

'Was It For This?' editorial, *Irish Times* 11 November 2010.

The *Irish Star* editorial, 24 August 2012.

Pat Rabbitte quote: *Eolas* Magazine, 13 May 2011.

Enda Kenny at Béal na mBláth, August 2012 Fine Gael website.

Geithner intervention: 'Ireland's future depends on breaking free from bailout', Morgan Kelly, *Irish Times*, 5 May 2011.

Michael Noonan: 'We left each other on the basis that I could ring him any time . . .' Transcript of interview by Richard Downes, RTÉ website.

'Grandmother (77) gets tasty treat with €2.6m Lotto win', Linda McGrory and Greg Harkin, *Irish Independent*, 5 December 2011.

'Undernourished child collapses', Eoin English and Fiachra Ó Cionnaith, *Irish Examiner*, 15 May 2012.

Michael Soden on *Tonight with Vincent Browne*: 'Lone parent remark sparks outrage', Scott Millar, *Irish Examiner*, 18 September 2009; and 'Banker who let slip mask of the elite', Gene Kerrigan, *Sunday Independent*, 20 September 2009.

Soden on extra half-day work for public servants: *Evening Herald*, 4 October 2010.

'Soden: Nama intervention would bring "wonderful factor of greed" back to property market', *BreakingNews.ie*, 16 August 2012.

Joe Little report on RTÉ: quoted in 'Latest ingenious way to save money', Gene Kerrigan, *Sunday Independent*, 16 October 2012.

'HSE withdraws call to use fewer incontinence pads', Fiona Gartland, *Irish Times*, 11 May 2012.

The Price of Offshore Revisited, report by Tax Justice Network, July 2012.

'UCC head's holiday home up for rent at €2,000 a week', Eoin English, *Irish Examiner*, 10 October 2012.

Editorial ('strain on patriotism'), *Irish Independent*, 3 January 2012.

John Bruton speaker profile, The London Speaker Bureau, and international speakers' page of Prime Performers.

'Bruton – I won't hand back my pension unless forced by law', Laura Noonan, *Irish Independent*, 5 January 2012.

Phil Hogan pension: 'Fine Gael deputy on €110,000 "can't take wage cut"', Aine Kerr, *Irish Independent*, 20 February 2009.

Mattie McGrath quote: 'Septic tank charge another "attack on rural Tipperary"', Dermot Keyes, *Munster Express*, 2 December 2011.

Michael Taft quote: Notes on the Front, 24 September 2012.

Judges' salaries, *Irish Independent* chart, quoted in 'Amazing adventures of People's Banker', Gene Kerrigan, 31 July 2011.

'Noonan Says He May Print "Ireland Is Not Greece" T-Shirts', Joe Brennan and Dara Doyle, Bloomberg.com, 23 June 2011.

Spotlight, No.5, 2011, Bulletin of the Oireachtas Library and Research Service, 2011, 'Tackling Social Welfare Fraud'.

SARP legislation: Carl O'Brien, *Irish Times*, 7 July 2012.

Drinks legislation: *The Corporate Takeover of Ireland*, Kieran Allen.

Michael McLoughlin quote: 'Under their influence: FF "gang" killed McDowell's cafe bar idea', Fionnan Sheahan, *Irish Independent*, 28 November 2005.

'Bill will stifle business – banker', *Irish Times*, 5 May 2003.

Michael Noonan, Dáil Éireann Debate, Vol. 725, No. 2, 15 December 2010.

Dominic Hannigan on *Tonight with Vincent Browne*, April 2012, YouTube: 'Vincent Browne Finally Admits Defeat'.

Vincent Browne and Klaus Masuch, January 2012, YouTube: 'Vincent Browne v The ECB'.

Oliver Wyman, 'World's best bank (2006 vintage)', Joseph Cotterill, FT/Alphaville, *Financial Times*, 11 February 2011.

'Our banks keep going back for more', Kathleen Barrington, *Sunday Business Post*, 6 December 2009.

'Property market's no house of cards', Ken McDonald, *Sunday Independent*, 25 March 2007.

'We need these expert scaremongers', Marc Coleman, *Sunday Independent*, 23 September 2007.

'Now is the right time to buy': YouTube, 'Donie Cassidy, FF Seanad Leader on house prices, Seanad Éireann, 10 April 2008'.

Philip Ingram/Merrill Lynch report: 'When Irish Eyes Are Crying', Michael Lewis, *Vanity Fair*, March 2011.

Peter Sutherland speech: 'Ireland is "talking itself into a crisis"', Niamh Hennessy, *Irish Examiner*, 5 April 2008.

'Celtic Tiger Sharpens its Claws for Recovery', Peter Sutherland, *Financial Times*, 12 April 2009.

ESRI in 2005, quoted in 'Our deluded ESRI', Adrian Kelleher, *Village* magazine, 7 June 2012.

ESRI in 2008, 'the fundamentals of the Irish economy are sound': *Medium Term Review 11, 2008 2015*, May 2008.

Peter Sutherland on *Morning Ireland*, 22 September 2011, quoted in 'Furthering inequality in divided society', Gene Kerrigan, *Sunday Independent*, 25 September 2011.

'What a disaster and an obscenity', Michael Noonan, Dáil Debates, Vol. 725, Wednesday, 15 December 2010.

Michael Burke statistics: TASC blog, 5 September 2012. www.progressive-economy.ie/2012/09/national-income-and-expenditure-2011.html

Quotes from Supachai Panitchpakdi and Heiner Flassbeck, United Nations Conference on Trade and Development (UNCTAD) report, September 2011, 'Post-crisis Policy Challenges in the World Economy'.

Gene Kerrigan was born and lives in Dublin, where he has covered politics, crime and scandals for over thirty years. He wrote for *Magill* magazine and the *Sunday Tribune*, and currently writes for the *Sunday Independent*. Among his non-fiction books are the best-selling *Hard Cases*, *Another Country* and *This Great Little Nation*. He's also the author of four novels, the latest of which, *The Rage*, won the UK's top crime fiction award, the Gold Dagger for Best Crime Novel, at the 2012 Crime Writers' Association awards.